To Charlie -

May this inspi[re]

much love,

[illegible]

Christmas, 2009

Art as a Way of Life

Edited and Illustrated by Roderick MacIver

Published by

North Atlantic Books
P.O. Box 12327
Berkeley, California 94712

and

Heron Dance Press and Art Studio
179 Rotax Road
North Ferrisburgh, Vermont 05743
888-304-3766
www.herondance.org

Cover art "Egret Away" and watercolors throughout are by Roderick MacIver of Heron Dance unless otherwise noted.

Printed in the United States of America

Art as a Way of Life is sponsored by the Society for the Study of Native Arts and Sciences, a nonprofit educational corporation whose goals are to develop an educational and cross-cultural perspective linking various scientific, social, and artistic fields; to nurture a holistic view of arts, sciences, humanities, and healing; and to publish and distribute literature on the relationship of mind, body, and nature.

North Atlantic Books' publications are available through most bookstores. For further information, visit our Web site at www.northatlanticbooks.com or call 800-733-3000.

Library of Congress Cataloging-in-Publication Data
Art as a way of life / edited by Roderick MacIver.
p. cm.
Summary: "Examines the rewards, joys, and challenges of the creative life through the words of artists, writers, poets, and musicians"--Provided by publisher.
ISBN 978-1-55643-920-9
1. Creation (Literary, artistic, etc.) 2. Creative ability. 3. Aesthetics. 4. Art--Philosophy. I. MacIver, Roderick.
BH301.C84A78 2009
702.3--dc22
2009039028

1 2 3 4 5 6 7 8 9 United 14 13 12 11 10 09

A work of art is the trace of a
magnificent struggle.
- Robert Henri, *The Art Spirit*

What I am actually saying is that we each need to let our intuition guide us, and then be willing to follow that guidance directly and fearlessly.

- Shakti Gawain

Contents

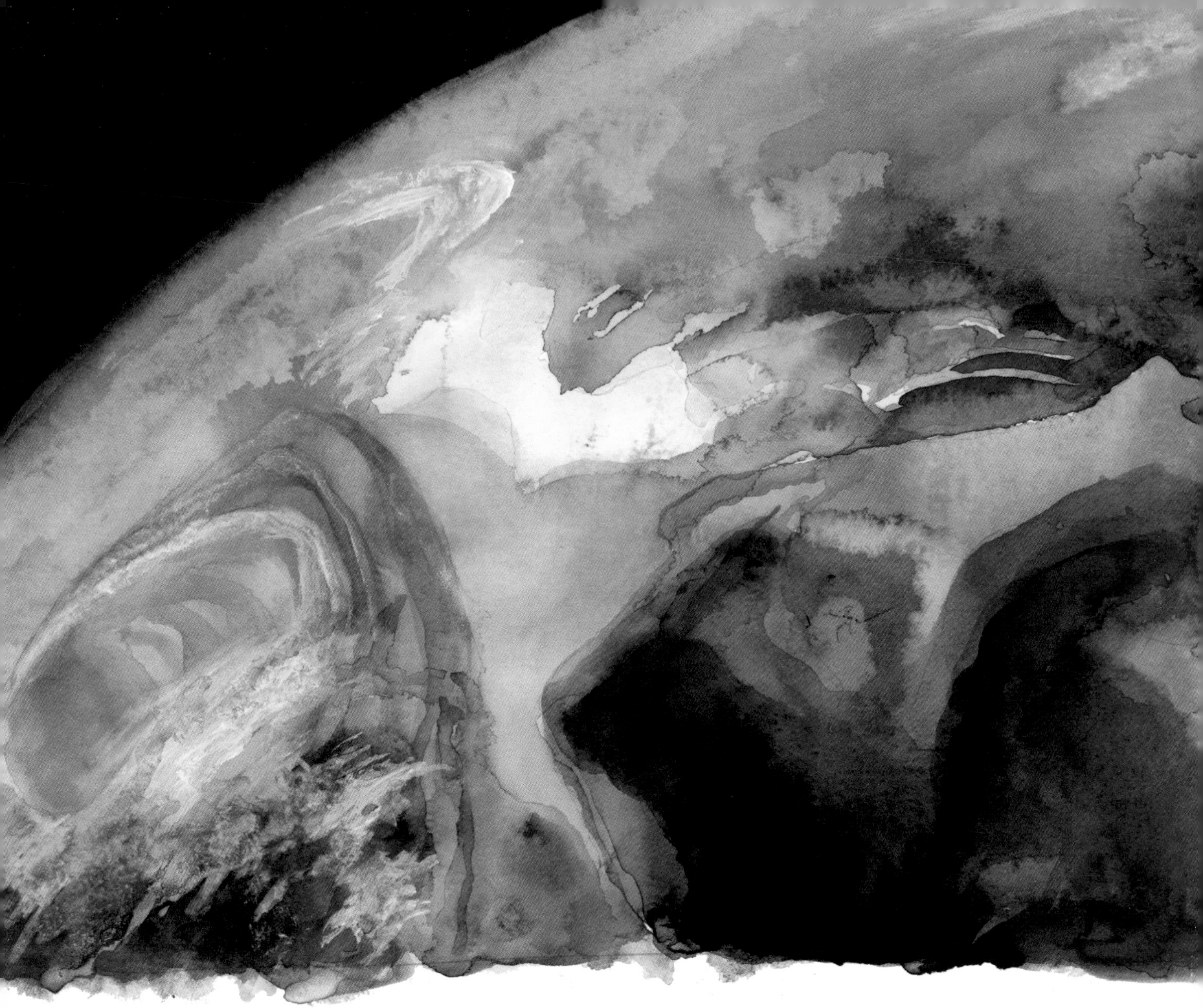

All art is a terrific bridge. The arts are not just entertainment. Music, paintings, words, they really do speak to the soul, to the heart, to the spirit, to each and every one of us human beings and members of this one tribe. Members of this one planet.

- Julia Cameron

Creation is still going on...the creative forces are as great and as active today as they have ever been...tomorrow's morning will be as heroic as any of the world. Creation is here and now. So near is man to the creative pageant, so much a part is he of the endless and incredible experiment, that any glimpse he may have will be but the revelation of a moment, a solitary note heard in a symphony thundering through debatable existence of time. Poetry is as necessary to comprehension as science. It is as impossible to live without reverence as it is without joy.

- Henry Beston, from *The Outermost House*

...a first-rate soup is more creative than a second-rate painting.

- Abraham Maslow

Introduction

Roderick MacIver

> **My father was very sure about certain matters pertaining to the universe. To him, all good things – trout as well as eternal salvation – come by grace and grace comes by art and art does not come easily.**
> **- Norman Maclean, from** *A River Runs Through It*

The ancient roots of the word "art" have to do with connection, and art, at its best, is our connection to the mystery, to the parts of ourselves that are deeper and truer than the day-to-day world. Art connects us to dreams, to the things that can't be explained with words, to the things that have touched our core, to imaginary worlds, and even to our personal chaos. Art has something to do with the part that doesn't want to be tamed, that can't be tamed.

Years ago, in *Birds in Art*, the annual catalog of the Leigh, Yawkey, Woodson Art Museum, I came across a couple of rough watercolor sketches that captured my imagination. They were very rough—they only vaguely resembled crows, their stated subject—but they were powerful. The accompanying note by the artist explained that she had suffered from depression all her life, and that she found solace and relief in art. I put those images on the wall of my studio as a reminder of how powerful art can be regardless of whether or not it bears a close resemblance to a particular physical form. Its power comes from a place deep in its creator and it registers somewhere deep in the viewer.

But this book is not just about being an artist, whatever that means. It is about an overall approach to life, a life that grows out of a close connection with a sacred center, with our inner world. To me, the phrases, "a life lived as art" or "art as a way of life" are about a thoughtful life, a life of grace. Kindness plays a role in that life, as does friendship and love. It embodies quiet humility, an acceptance of the way things are. Sometimes, art is the manifestation of living in close contact with a sacred center. Sometimes life as art manifests itself in other, equally beautiful, ways.

Living art as a way of life is a result of careful thought. It requires a plan and dedication. Without nurturing, the connection with our inner world withers and fades away. Then the culture around us sneaks in and takes over. We don't want that. The culture around us is complicated and rushed.

Artists and writers—at least those who create a formidable body of work—tend to have a practice that allows them to "make contact" with the source of their creative life. It generally has something to do with slowing down, with quiet.

The ancient roots of the word "art" have to do with connection, and art, at its best, is our connection to the mystery, to the parts of ourselves that are deeper and truer than the day-to-day world. Art connects us to dreams, to the things that can't be explained with words, to the things that have touched our core, to imaginary worlds, and even to our personal chaos. Art has something to do with the part that doesn't want to be tamed, that can't be tamed.

Years ago, in *Birds in Art*, the annual catalog of the Leigh, Yawkey, Woodson Art Museum, I came across a couple of rough watercolor sketches that captured my imagination. They were very rough—they only vaguely resembled crows, their stated subject—but they were powerful. The accompanying note by the artist explained that she had suffered from depression all her life, and that she had found solace and relief in art. I put those images on the wall of my studio as a reminder of how powerful art can be regardless of whether or not it bears a close resemblance to a particular physical form. Its power comes from a place deep in its creator and it registers somewhere deep in the viewer.

But this book is not just about being an artist, whatever that means. It is about an overall approach to life, a life that grows out of a close connection with a sacred center, with our inner world. To me, the phrases, "a life lived as art" or "art as a way of life" are about a thoughtful life, a life of grace. Kindness plays a role in that life, as does friendship and love. It embodies quiet humility, an acceptance of the way things are. Sometimes, art is the manifestation of living in close contact with a sacred center. Sometimes life as art manifests itself in other, equally beautiful, ways.

Living art as a way of life is a result of careful thought. It requires a plan and dedication. Without nurturing, the connection with our inner world withers and fades away. Then the culture around us sneaks in and takes over. We don't want that. The culture around us is complicated and rushed.

Artists and writers—at least those who create a formidable body of work—tend to have a practice that allows them to "make contact" with the source of their creative life. It generally has something to do with slowing down, with quiet.

> ...that best portion of a good man's life,
> His little, nameless, unremembered acts
> Of kindness and of love.
>
> - William Wordsworth

> I always get up and make a cup of coffee while it is still dark—it must be dark—and then I drink the coffee and watch the light come... Writers all devise ways to approach that place where they expect to make the contact, where they become the conduit, or where they engage in this mysterious process. For me, light is the signal in the transition. It's not being in the light, it's being there before it arrives. It enables me, in some sense.
>
> - Toni Morrison

I come home to my solitary woodland walk as the homesick go home. I thus dispose of the superfluous and see things as they are, grand and beautiful.

- Henry David Thoreau, in his journal, January 1857

I've read and re-read Thoreau's work for almost forty years, and of everything I've read, the excerpt that challenges me most asks us to make our lives works of art. The following quote from Walden was the early inspiration for this book.

It is something to be able to paint a particular picture, or to carve a statue, and so to make a few objects beautiful, but it is more glorious to carve and paint the very atmosphere and medium through which we look, which morally we can do. To affect the quality of the day, that is the highest of arts. We are tasked to make our lives, even in its details, worthy of the contemplation of our most elevated and critical hour.

- Henry David Thoreau, *Walden*

The ultimate is a life in which the person we are, the way we live and conduct ourselves nurtures a work of love, and vice versa. I come to this subject not as an accomplished expert but as a person who tries and sometimes fails. Art, as difficult as it is to create, is easier than living a life that is a work of art. My repeated failing is trying to do too much. I've repeatedly pushed the limits passed the point of my energy and financial resources. At times, this has led to a kind of desperation.

It is a characteristic of wisdom not to do desperate things.

- Thoreau

A life lived as art, and a life lived in desperation, are at opposite ends of the spectrum. Wisdom comes from experience, and experience comes from failure. Or something like that. A life lived as art has an element of reserve built into its design. It balances striving for goals, accomplishments and adventures with time for quiet and peace. It is a life that above all grows out of a sacred center. An artist, to create work that is profound, that is powerful, must have and nurture a deep, close relationship with his or her inner world. The same is true of the non-artist seeking to live a harmonious, balanced life.

Much of this book explores artists' thoughts on living in a way that nurtures our relationship with our subconscious mind. We do that with downtime, with silence and time alone. We can do it through meditation, prayer, long hot baths, bicycle rides in the country. We can do it by sitting in a quiet room with a pencil and paper asking ourselves questions while meditating, and writing down the answers we get. Sometimes the answers we get back can't be understood. Still, we try to maintain and develop the lines of communication with our repository. It is shy.

There are moments in our lives, there are moments in a day, when we seem to see beyond the usual—become clairvoyant. We reach then into reality. Such are the moments of our greatest happiness. Such are the moments of our greatest wisdom.

It is in the nature of all people to have these experiences; but in our time and under the conditions of our lives, it is only a rare few who are able to continue in the experience and find expression for it.

At such times there is a song going on within us, a song to which we listen. It fills us with surprise. We marvel at it. We would continue to hear it. But few are capable of holding themselves in the state of listening to their song. Intellectuality steps in and, as the song within us is of the utmost sensitiveness, it retires in the presence of the cold, material intellect. It is aristocratic and will not associate itself with the commonplace—and we fall back and become our ordinary selves. Yet we live in the memory of these songs which in moments of intellectual inadvertence have been possible to us. They are the pinnacles of our experience and it is the desire to express these intimate sensations, this song from within, which motivates the masters of all art.

- Robert Henri from *The Art Spirit*

It is often easy to turn our back on the song within, on the interior silence and interior chaos. It is easy, but we're poorer for it. When we turn our back on our gift, we turn our back on life. It's easy to have interests but whatever you give your heart to will challenge your being on the most profound levels.

To dive down, find the beauty, nurture it and offer it to the world is magnificent. Staying with your beauty, your truth, your integrity is difficult, but out of these things comes meaning, and meaning is all-transcendent.

To create something out of one's soul and one's love—a handmade ceramic teacup, a painting, a carving, a magnificent soup or beautiful garden—has the power to nourish other souls that are open to work of love. And people who are open to work of love tend to be people who get bumped around a lot by this world. Their goodwill needs support, and they find it in places as diverse as a sunset, a piece of music or art, or a handmade wooden bowl of simplicity and elegance.

I think of my art as, in part, an effort to nurture the best that is in me. I want those places of my soul to gradually take over my life, my interactions, my relationship with myself. To the extent it succeeds, the work is greater than I am, more honest than I am, more beautiful than I am. I work for the day, perhaps unattainable, when it all merges together.

What is life?

It is the flash of a firefly in the night.
It is the breath of a buffalo in the winter time;
It is the little shadow which runs across the grass
and loses itself in the sunset.

- Last words of Crowfoot, Blackfoot hunter

The challenge of expressing, through painting, my deepest loves, my most profound experiences, most of which have occurred in wild places, is the challenge and inspiration of my life.

We can copy others, we can live to please others, or we can discover that which is unique and precious to us, and paint that, become that. It is a task which takes a lifetime.

-Carl Rogers

Chapter One

Your Inner World: The Repository of Creativity

Creative people are especially observant, and they value accurate observation (telling themselves the truth) more than other people do. They often express part truths, but this they do vividly, the part they express is the generally unrecognized; by displacement of accent and apparent disproportion in statement they seem to point to the usually unobserved... They have more contact than most people do with the life of the unconscious—with fantasy, with reverie, the world of imagination.

- David Olgilvy from *Confessions of an Advertising Man*

No great work has ever been produced except after a long interval of still and musing meditation.

- Walter Begehot

Construction on a purely spiritual basis is a slow business... The artist must train not only his eye but also his soul...

- Wassily Kandinsky

The outward work will never be puny if the inward work is great.

- Meister Eckhart

To paint is not to copy the object slavishly, it is to grasp a harmony among many relationships.

- Paul Cézanne

Art seems to me to be a state of soul more than anything else. The soul of all is sacred.

- Marc Chagall

What I was after is what you get sugaring off maple from the maple tree. You keep boiling it down until you have the essence of purity.

- Andrew Wyeth

For my part, I declare I know nothing whatever about it, but looking at the stars always makes me dream, as simply as I dream over the black dots representing towns and villages on a map. I ask myself, shouldn't the shining dots of the sky be as accessible as the black dots on the map of France? Just as we take the train to get to Tarascon or Rouen, we take death to reach a star. One thing undoubtedly true in this reasoning is this: that while we are alive we cannot get to a star, any more than when we are dead we can take the train.

So it doesn't seem impossible to me that cholera, gravel, pleurisy & cancer are the means of celestial locomotion, just as steam-boats, omnibuses and railways are the terrestrial means. To die quietly of old age would be to go there on foot.

- Vincent Van Gogh in a letter to his brother Theo, July 1888

I am almost incapable of logical thought, but I have developed techniques for keeping open the telephone line to my unconscious, in case that disorderly repository has anything to tell me. I hear a great deal of music. I am on friendly terms with John Barleycorn. I take long hot baths. I garden. I go into retreat among the Amish. I watch birds. I go for long walks in the country. And I take frequent vacations so that my brain can lie fallow—no golf, no cocktail parties, no tennis, no bridge, no concentration, only a bicycle.

- David Ogilvy, from *Confessions of an Advertising Man*

Cornelius Vanderbuilt, in his big transactions, seemed to act almost on impulse and intuition. He could never explain the mental processes by which he arrived at important decisions, though these decisions by themselves were invariably sound. He seems to have had, as he himself had frequently said, a seer-like faculty. He saw visions and believed in dreams and signs. The greatest practical genius of his time was a frequent attendant at spiritualistic séances; he cultivated personally the society of mediums, and in sickness he usually resorted to mental healers, mesmerists, and clairvoyants. Before making investments or embarking on his great railroad ventures, Vanderbuilt visited spiritualists; we have one circumstantial picture of his summoning the wraith of Jim Fisk to advise him in stock operations.

Creativity and intuition are double edges of the same sword, and a particular trait of the creative individual is his ability to disappear inside his head. A creative executive can sometimes seem as deaf and distraught as Beethoven when, stone deaf, he created the Ninth Symphony. Such a gift is not always endearing or recognized, and the early life of extremely successful executives commonly reveals a history of "delinquency": an unwillingness, sometimes an inability to submit to authority or to conform.

- John Wareham, from *Secrets Of A Corporate Headhunter*

A person's life purpose is nothing more than to rediscover, through the detours of art, or love, or passionate work, those one or two images in the presence of which his heart first opened.

-Albert Camus

Art is not a luxury! Art arises from one's depths or it is not art but kitsch! Art, for me, is and was my digging tool for Meaning, for Truth...my own truth that may speak to your truth. Art then becomes a "religious," a spiritual act, not in any sectarian sense but as a witness to a "religious" attitude to sheer being, to existence as such, being Supremely Meaningful.

- Frederick Franck, from the booklet *Pacem In Terris,* describing their peace gardens: "a sacred place that speaks to the sacred space at the core of the human heart."

For original ideas to come about, you have to let them percolate under the level of consciousness in a place where we have no way to make them obey our own desires or our own direction. Their random combinations are driven by forces we don't know about.

- Mihalyi Csikszentmihalyi, author of *Flow: The Psychology of Optimal Experience*

It is what is left over when everything explainable has been explained that makes a story worth writing and reading. The writer's gaze has to extend beyond the surface, beyond mere problems, until it touches that realm of mystery which is the concern of prophets....If a writer believes that the life of a man is and will remain essentially mysterious, what he sees on the surface, or what he understands, will be of interest to him only as it leads him into the experience of mystery itself.

- Flannery O'Connor, Literary Witch, from *Colorado Quarterly* (Spring 1962)

It took Jean Giono 23 years to write, rethink and rewrite *The Man Who Planted Trees.* That effort and elapse of time is crucial to the creation of all great art, Frederic says. "It is fantastic to spend a long time creating a work of art. The search for beauty is without end. To make a kind of physic work you need time to reflect and rework. When you come to the end, you see the beginning differently. Time is not money. Time is our most precious possession. No money can buy time. The message of Jean Giono's book also touches on that—with time comes power. We can use it to improve or to destroy."

- Frédéric Back, HERON DANCE interview, Issue 1.

We have to be able to be gods, lovers, and artists, we have to be soulful if we're going to be happy, if we want peace—and the soul is the part of us that is the creative process. And how do we access those soulful states of being as opposed to the ego state of being, and how do we know the difference? These are real questions, and they're the ones that have driven me. What does it mean to be a human being? That's the initial question for me. What does it really mean? I'm still working on that question.

- Gabrielle Roth, from
Wild Heart Journal

Robertson Davies, the Canadian author, said one of the most important things in his life was being able to take a nap every day after lunch for twenty minutes. That's for two reasons. One is that by developing a schedule that's under your control, you are not being flogged around by life, as he puts it; you are not always jumping to someone else's tune. You develop your own rhythm of work and rest. The other thing is that it's during idle time that ideas have a chance to recombine in new ways, because if we think consciously about solving a problem or writing a book, then we are sitting there forcing our ideas to move in a lockstep, in a straight line, and probably what comes out is not very new or original.

- Mihalyi Csikszentmihalyi
in a Michael Toms interview

We are all wounded inside in some way or other.
We all carry unhappiness within us for some reason or another.
Which is why we need a little gentleness and healing from
one another. Healing in words, healing beyond words.
Like gestures. Warm gestures. Like friendship, which will always
Be like a mystery. Like a smile, which someone described
As the shortest distance between two people.

- Ben Okri, from the poem
Healing The Wounded Learner
or the Pygmalion Complex

Yes, the highest things are beyond words.

That is probably why all art aspires to the condition of wordlessness. When literature works on you, it does so in silence, in your dreams, in your wordless moments. Good words enter you and become moods, become the quiet fabric of your being. Like music, like painting, literature, too, wants to transcend its primary condition and become something higher. Art wants to move into silence, into the emotional and spiritual conditions of the world. Statues become melodies, melodies become yearnings, yearnings become actions.

- Ben Okri, from the book
A Way of Being Free

An essential portion of any artist's labor is not creation so much as invocation. Part of the work cannot be made, it must be received; and we cannot have this gift except, perhaps, by supplication, by courting, by creating within ourselves that "begging bowl" to which the gift is drawn.

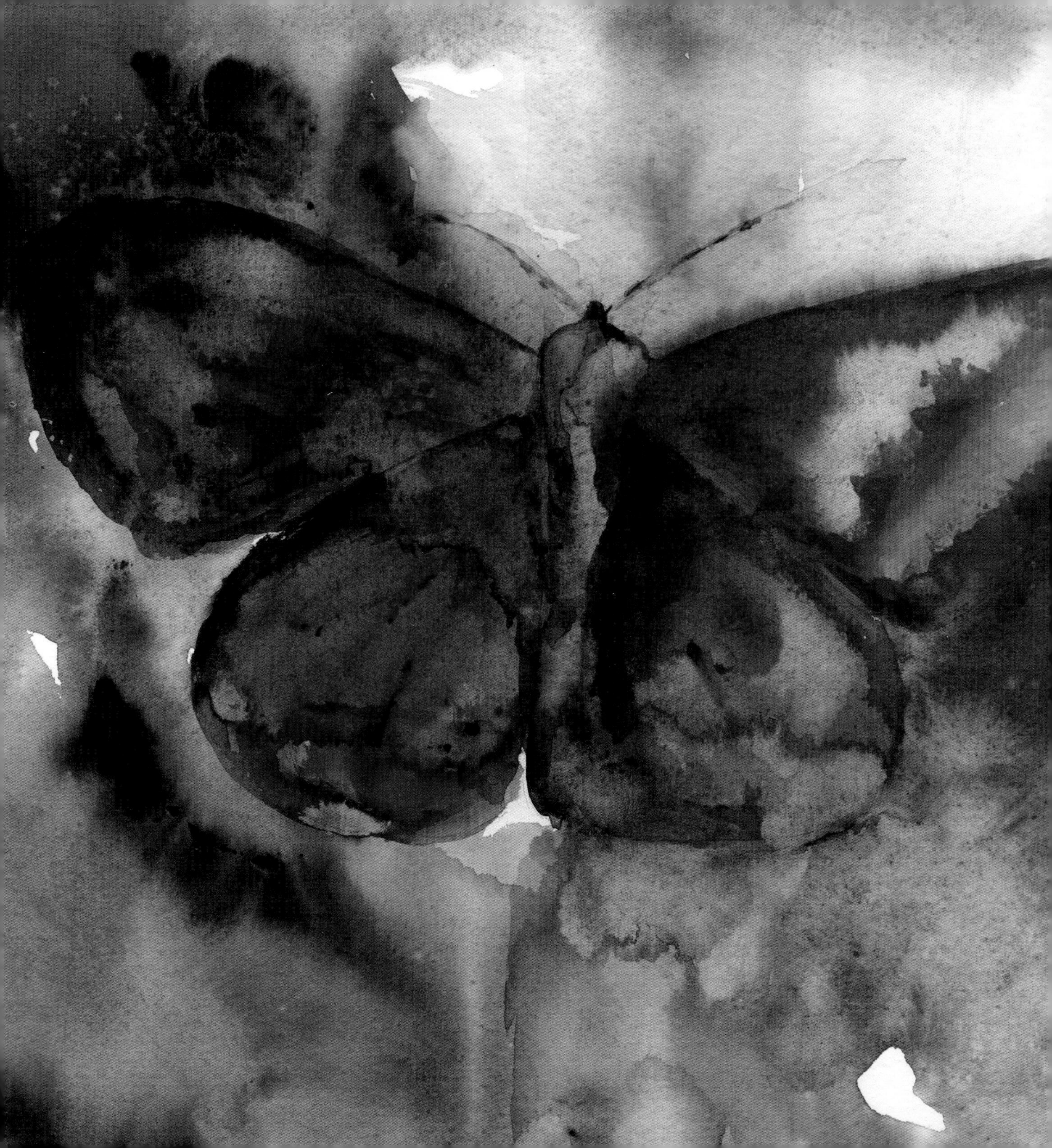

May all things move and be moved in me

and know and be known in me

May all creation

dance for joy within me

- Chinook Psalter

I think the real artists are too busy with just being and growing and acting (on canvas or however) like themselves to worry about the end. The end will be what it will be. The object is intense living, fulfillment; the great happiness in creation.

- Robert Henri, from *The Art Spirit*

The great German author Thomas Mann wrote, "Art is the spirit in matter, the natural instinct toward humanization, that is, toward the spiritualization of life..." [This instinct] provides a bridge uniting the fine and the practical arts, the spiritual life with the art of creative living...

This concept unites the work of Gandhi with the Japanese tea ceremony, the mission work of Albert Schweitzer with Mozart's Magic Flute, Navaho sand painting with the great cathedrals of Europe, the work of Mother Teresa with that of Goethe, the poetry of the troubadours with the scriptures of India, the work of Albert Einstein with that of the anonymous but devoted local elementary school teacher. All of these are art because they spring from what Mann calls the natural instinct toward humanization.

- Laurence G. Boldt, from
Zen and the Art of Making a Living

At my place, I've begun to have little recognitions of things that have been there all along but I haven't noticed them before. They come clear in a different way than they do when you simply go out and study them. There's a big, old live oak down in one end of the meadow I have walked by hundreds of times. I knew what it was—an interior live oak. I've crawled under it on several occasions. It was no mystery to me. But one day last spring, I stopped and took a look at it, and I really saw it. In a sense, it showed itself to me. No woo-woo about it. It wasn't anything particularly magical or anything, it's just that I really saw it. I could see that it was very old and that it had been through maybe one full fire that had burned it down, its base thickened by a rebuilt root stalk. Its wonderfully complex arm structure was sheltering a horde of birds. I saw these forms as though for the first time.

It's a gift; it's like there's a moment in which the thing is ready to let you see it. In India, this is called *darshan*. Darshan means getting a view, and if the clouds blow away, as they did once for me, and you get a view of the Himalayas from the foothills, an Indian person would say, "Ah, the Himalayas are giving you their darshan;" they're letting you have their view. This comfortable, really deep way of getting a sense of something takes time. It doesn't show itself to you right away.

It isn't even necessary to know the names of things the way a botanist would. It's more important to be aware of the suchness of the thing; it's a reality. It's also a source of a certain kind of inspiration for creativity. I see it in the work of Georgia O'Keeffe. She had that eye, you know.

- *Gary Snyder,* interviewed by Jonathan White, *Talking on the Water*

May the blessing of light be on you, light without and light within. May the blessed sunshine shine on you and warm your heart till it glows like a great peat fire, so that the stranger may come and warm himself at it, and also a friend.

- Traditional Irish Blessing

Chapter Two: *The Very Human Urge to Create*

Sometimes, I may do a painting that takes several months and when it is finished, I am exhausted. Then the very next day I will get an idea or a notion about wanting to do something, and do it spontaneously, and hit it right on the nose.

Once I was talking to Robert Frost about a poem of his that is so beautifully written, it is considered by some to be actually perfect. It is called "Stopping by Woods on a Snowy Evening." And I asked him, "You must have worked a long time on that. It must have been done in the middle of the winter. What was your experience?" He said, 'Andy, I'll tell you about that. I'd been writing a very complicated, long-drawn-out poem, almost a story type of poem entitled 'Death of a Hired Man.' I had finished at two o'clock in the morning. It was a hot August night, and I was exhausted. I walked out on the porch of my house and looked at the mountain range. It came to me in a flash! I wrote it on an envelope I had in my pocket, and I only changed one word. It came out just like that."

- Thomas Hoving, *The Two Worlds of Andrew Wyeth*

[Art] is an attempt to find in its forms, in its colors, in its light, in its shadows, in the aspects of matter and in the fact of life what of each is enduring and essential—their one illuminating and convincing quality—the very truth of their existence. The artist, then, like the thinker or the scientist, seeks the truth and makes his appeal... His appeal is made to our less obvious capabilities, to that part of our nature which, because of the warlike conditions of existence, is necessarily kept out of sight within the more resisting and hard qualities—like the vulnerable body within steel armor. His appeal is less loud, more profound, less distinct, more stirring—and sooner forgotten. Yet its effect endures forever. [The artist's] task is to make you hear, to make you feel—it is, before all, to make you see. That—and no more and it is everything.

- Joseph Conrad

I believe one has to stop holding back for fear of alienating some imaginary reader or real relative or friend and come out with personal truth. If we are to understand the human condition, and if we are to accept ourselves in all the complexity, self-doubt, extravagance of feeling, guilt, joy, the slow freeing of the self to its full capacity for action and creation, both as human being and as artist, we have to know all we can about each other, and we have to be willing to go naked.

- May Sarton

This is what I learned: that everybody is talented, original, and has something important to say. Everybody is talented because everybody who is human has something to express. Everybody is original, if she tells the truth, if she speaks from herself. But it must be from her true self and not the self she thinks she should be. So remember these two things: you are talented and you are original. Be sure of that. I say this because self-trust is one of the very most important things in writing.

- Brenda Ueland

There is a vitality, a life force, a quickening
That is translated through you into action,
And because there is only one of you in all time,
This expression is unique.

And if you block it,
It will never exist through any other medium
And be lost.
The world will not have it.
It is not your business to determine how good it is,
Nor how valuable it is, nor how it compares with other expressions.
It is your business to keep it yours clearly and directly,
To keep the channel open.

You do not even have to believe in yourself or your work.
You have to keep open and aware directly
To the urges that motivate you.

Keep the channel open.
No artist is ever pleased.
There is no satisfaction whatever at any time.
There is only a queer, divine satisfaction,
A blessed unrest that keeps us marching
And makes us more alive than the others.

- Martha Graham

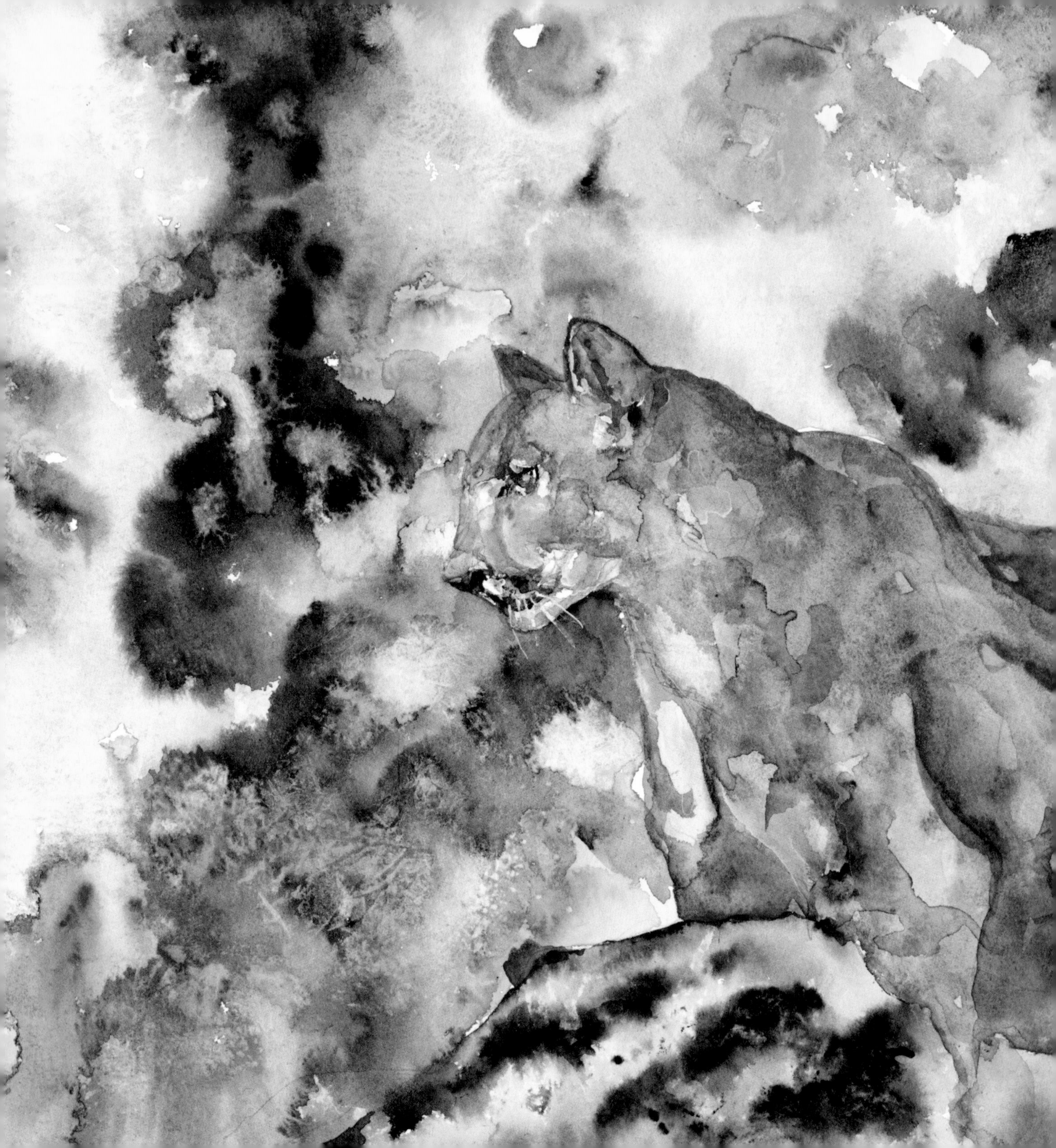

All my work is transformative. Always has been. That's what work does when the work emanates from the mind. From the heart. But how it changed my inner life—my spiritual life, if you like—is an altogether different issue. On the surface there is very little change. I am still as much of a reprobate as I have ever been—a man who, as Benjamin Franklin said, can fart proudly. Can cuss. Can belch. And can spit natural juices and watermelon seeds with the best of them. I can be, and am from time to time, as sacrilegious, as bawdy, and as profane, perhaps, as those miscreants I placed at the foot of the cross. In many superficial ways I am no better than they. Underneath, though, this work brought me back to a familiar old struggle, one I had given up. A struggle with God, I suppose you would call it. Or with the idea of God. My struggle with the dichotomy of profanity and beauty. It has certainly made me less reticent to mention God in my conversations. I am Peter Scaffer's flawed Amadeus when he said to Joseph II, "Your Grace, It is true what the cappellmiester says. I am a profane man, but I assure you, sire, my work is not."

- Barry Moser from his essay *Tenkh & Testament*

Transformative art must express something beyond where you are, it demands that you grow beyond your current self. This is where an artist's angst and the pain of transformation coincide. You reach toward the true, the good and the beautiful and become a better person through the struggle.

- Alex Grey, artist (alexgrey.com)

The spiritual journey is a creative journey. It's about birth. It calls us past the boundaries of convention. It tests our willingness to see life in a new way and our courage to express it: for new ways of viewing life in the face of what is commonly accepted. We become new, and in this ongoing birthing, we bring new forms to life as well. Life itself has become a creative act, full of vitality and richness and passion.

- Anne Hillman, from *Dancing Animal Woman*

Some say the creative life is in ideas, some say it is in doing. It seems in most instances to be in simply being. It is not virtuosity, although that is very fine in itself. It is the love of something, having so much love for something—whether a person, a word, an image, an idea, the land, or humanity—that all that can be done with the overflow is to create. It is not a matter of wanting to, not a singular act of will; one solely must.

- Clarissa Pinkola Estés, from *Women Who Run with the Wolves*

I rarely arrive at an idea by consciously sitting down at a desk and trying to figure out what I want to do. Once I start thinking about a project, though, it doesn't leave my focus until I have come up with an idea.

I cannot force a design; I do not see this process as being under my conscious control. It is a process of percolation, with the form eventually finding its way to the surface.

- Maya Lin, designer of the Vietnam Veterans Memorial, from *Boundaries*

All I can go with is my personal truth, my integrity, and my intuition. I try to tap everyday into that higher voice that I hear and trust. That is more than enough. I feel good when coming from that place. If I don't come from that place, I get lost in the darkness and the despair. You cannot know what the outcome is supposed to be. We cannot be goal-orientated. We have to believe that if we do the very best that we can, and practice harmony with each other and with the Earth, that something larger will be served, though we may not see it...we may not see it.

- Cielo Myczack, from Issue 4 of HERON DANCE

Tom Jay—Sculptor

Heron Dance interview by Roderick MacIver

Tom Jay has worked as a salmon fisherman, a bronze foundry operator, and for the last seven years, as a sculptor. He lives with his wife Mall, also a sculptor, on the Olympic Peninsula of Washington State in a funky pole house they built in the '70s. A lot of what Tom says has to do with serving a place—the soul of a place, the ghosts of a place. He does this with his art, and he does it with efforts to restore the salmon run to the Chimacum Creek near where he lives. I asked him for his thoughts on beauty.

Beauty happens unexpectedly, but it comes out of a practice of attention and humility. And beauty is always a surprise. You can't go expecting beauty. It comes from tilling those fields. It comes practicing that practice, staying in the place. Because it is a deep thing. It is not a superficial thing. It is not expressive. It comes out of a tilth. It comes out of a depth. It comes out of your grandmother laughing at you from the grave. It comes out of remembering something far away in the past about a dog. It is unexpected and coiled up in us. And those little joints that the artist offers can sometimes invite beauty into the world because they are part of that practice. They are part of making those little nexus points. Beauty is surprise that is latent in the world. It takes imagination to catalyze it, but it is not something that we can control or demand. It invites us.

That is why sometimes those little Japanese Raku pots are really beautiful. Great skill, great learning, and tradition, and then the artist hopes and prays for the accident that will make it beautiful. How do you attend the calling without getting in the way? God blowing through your horn. It sounds a certain way, but you don't want to focus on the horn, you want to focus on the tune. A lot of artists, myself included, have a tendency to polish the horn, rather than play the tune. My work goes in and out of connection to the degree that I manipulate it. Rather than attend it.

The whole notion of beauty has come to be relative: "Beauty is in the eye of the beholder." I say, bullshit. Beauty is in itself. If two people can't recognize beauty together, we are in deep kimchee. Something is really wrong. For me, beauty is something in and of itself. Beauty can happen anywhere, anytime, any place. It can be the way the deer disappears into the birch glade. It can be a little kid. It can be made too.

It's a great relief to me to know that I can actually be creative and be happy at the same time.

- James W. Hall

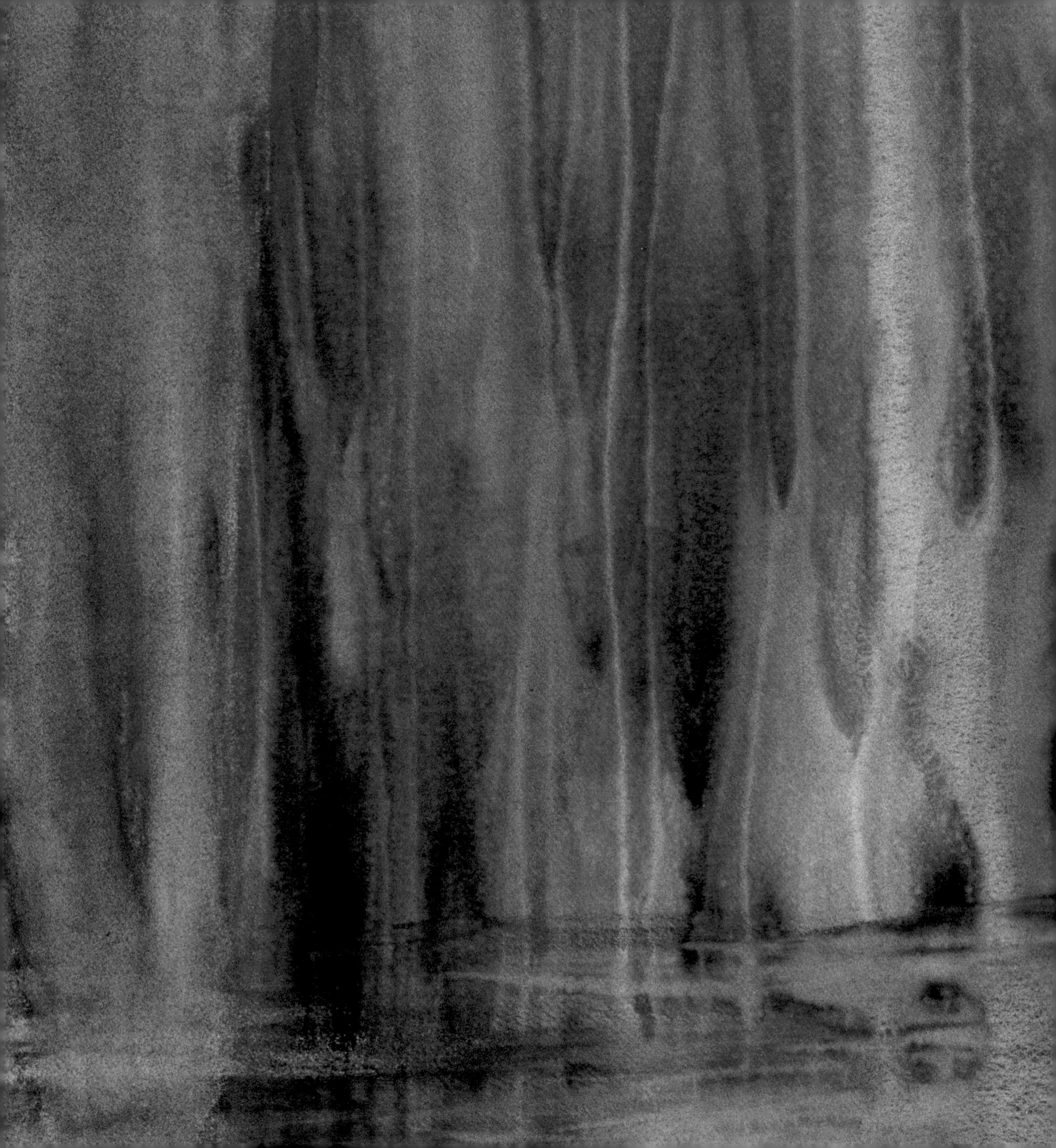

Chapter Three:

The Importance of Not Being Sure

A man should learn to watch that gleam of light which flashes across his mind from within, more than the luster of the firmament, of bards and sages. Yet he dismisses without notice his thought, because it is his. In every work of genius we recognize our own thoughts: they come back to us with a certain alienated majesty. Great works of art have no more abiding lesson for us than this. They teach us to abide by our own spontaneous impression with good-natured inflexibility when the whole cry of voices is on the other side.

- Ralph Waldo Emerson

Until I get wherever it is I am going, I want to nurture those corners of my psyche and soul that are peaceful and beautiful. I want my work to arise out of those places. I want my life to flow out of those places. It is surprisingly difficult to do that. It requires a confrontation with myself, a discipline over myself. When I sit down to paint, a thousand distractions beckon—unreturned phone messages, unpaid bills, unreconciled bank statements, dirty dishes, etc. However satisfying it is to complete a painting that comes out of that place of peace and beauty, that expresses my feelings about wild places and wild things, disappointment and discouragement are the more common outcome. In a strange way, it is more comfortable to do our bookkeeping. The process of making art is a process of confronting oneself, one's lack of talent, one's lack of confidence. It is what Robert Henri called "the magnificent struggle" in his excellent book *The Art Spirit*. In some ways it is like meditation. Art involves a confrontation with oneself that can be surprisingly uncomfortable.

- Roderick MacIver

Perfection is overrated. Sometimes it is the flawed, the damaged, the hapless that gives a piece its soul. If I welcome mistakes they often bring good news; a new way of thinking, a new way of seeing. When it seems as if nothing is working out as I had expected, I tell myself that, after all, it is only marks on a sheet of paper. Somehow this frees me up to see what my preconceived idea had disallowed.

Last year, Gail Berkus and I had beaten some abaca fiber in her new Hollander. Overbeating abaca produces a translucent paper that catches the sunlight like melted wax and sounds like the crackle of autumn. We miscalculated and beat the fiber way too long. Instead of the usual two to four minutes, this porridge-like slurry took 20 minutes per sheet to drain! An unending El Niño rainstorm kept me from making paper in my improvised outdoor studio. If the pulp sat much longer it would simply spoil, so I decided to just give in to the situation and make paper outdoors, in the rain. I made the weirdest, rain-spit paper I'd ever seen. It puckered and wrinkled as it dried, complete with the pentimento of a drizzly afternoon. Yet there is an uncanny beauty to it. Out of my control, I watched as something emerged out of mistake and mishap.

I used this abaca paper that I made by hand and let air dry, with all its irregularities and imperfections, to make this series of drawings based on Cycladic figures. The elemental intrusion onto the paper's surface of air and even raindrops became a counterpoint to the unwavering stance of the Cycladic form. For some, such as Delos, I burnished ochre pigment into the leathery surfaces.

- Mary Heebner, from
www.maryheebner.com

Sy Safransky—Editor of The Sun Magazine

Heron Dance interview by Roderick MacIver

Sy Safransky, founder and editor of The Sun, *has been a friend of mine and a friend of* Heron Dance *almost since we started—since the time when* Heron Dance *didn't have many friends. He is a man of truly good heart. When I interviewed Sy, he talked about the early days of* The Sun. *He showed me a photograph of himself 25 years ago—long hair and bare feet—selling The Sun on the streets of Chapel Hill for 25 cents a copy. For the first ten years of* The Sun's *existence, Sy lived on $100 a week. I asked Sy if his $100 salary was fairly reliable.*

There was a period when *The Sun* couldn't even pay me the $100 a week, so I worked for a friend's landscape company digging ditches and shoveling manure. But for the most part, I was able to get by.

Did you ever think of quitting?

I would get discouraged. I had never before had to juggle debt. Most of our creditors were patient and believed that I would eventually pay them off… At one point I owed the printer for eight back issues, and I had to pay him at least $500 before he'd print the next issue. The day before the new issue was ready someone sent in a $500 donation. Moments like that would occur with enough regularity to remind me that, in addition to the hard work that was keeping everything together, there was a quality of grace.

We can't insist on grace. Aldus Huxley once said that all you can do is tidy up your room, make everything as orderly and peaceful as you can, then open your window. You can't know when the breeze will blow in. But when it does blow in, you are ready. You are centered in that place, and you can experience the breeze.

I have seen that work in my own life and in other people's lives. If we do what we genuinely feel we must do, and we do it with integrity, the universe responds. It can't be reduced to a formula. I think that is a mistake that is often made in a lot of the writing about prosperity consciousness. But there is a seed of truth in that thinking, as long as it doesn't become overly

simplified and gimmicky. I have found that it has been helpful to be as conscious as I can about what my beliefs are.

The Sun went through a real transition a few years ago from constantly being broke to being able to pay its bills in a reasonably timely manner. First I had to go through a change on an inner level. I had to examine my attachment to being broke. It was in part a political statement. I did not want to be identified with people who were successful. I distrusted it. I thought wealth was corrupting. I used to think that if *The Sun* became successful, it would be the equivalent of some kind of loss of integrity. Although I was committed to the survival of the magazine, and was therefore willing to do whatever it took to keep it going, success frightened me.

What I've discovered, to my surprise and great relief, was that *The Sun*'s success hasn't compromised anything. Being able to pay the bills, and pay authors, or drive a car that isn't always breaking down is a blessing, not a cop-out.

I walked away from a well-paying newspaper job into what became involuntary poverty. Had I known what I was doing, I probably wouldn't have done it. So that's good. That sense of mystery about what we are getting into is really necessary. With relationships, with magazines, with everything. Maybe we wouldn't take birth if we knew what we are getting into. Maybe naïveté is necessary at the beginning of the journey. I don't know.

- Sy Safransky, from a
HERON DANCE Interview

There is always some accident in the best things, whether thoughts or expressions or deeds. The memorable thought, the happy expression, the admirable deed are only partly ours. The thought came to us because we were in a fit mood; also we were unconscious and did not know that we had said or done a good thing. We must walk consciously only part way toward our goal, and then leap in the dark to our success.

- Henry David Thoreau, from his journal

Everyone was finding their way. I was not interested in a strictly professional setup. I did not want to contain my talents in that box, because I didn't know where they were going to lead me at that time. At that time, my concern was this: I have these abilities, I don't know what they are, but I know that they are there. I don't know where they are going to lead me, but wherever that is, I have to go, even if it is down a bunch of blind alleys, until I find one that I do want to go down. Give me room to do this particular thing. In my own fashion.

The primary questions that I would be writing about for the rest of my work life first took form in the songs on *Born To Run*. What do you do when your dreams come true? What do you do when they don't? Is love real? *Born to Run* was the album where I left behind my adolescent definitions of love and freedom. It was the real dividing line.

- Bruce Springsteen, from
the movie "Born to Run"

Frédéric Back—Artist

Heron Dance interview by Roderick MacIver

Frédéric Back is a humble and brilliant Québécois artist whose art and life have been a source of great inspiration to me. His animated film "The Man Who Planted Trees" won an Academy Award in 1998. It took him five years to draw the 20,000 images for the film.

Most of what I do, I do by an instinct that I cannot explain. There are many artists who speak well of art and philosophy and that kind of thing; when you see what they create, it is often disappointing. It is not rich. They are better speakers than they are artists. I taught for five years and was very uneasy about speaking about art. I had no beautiful theory. No fantastic explanation about art. Art for me is just a natural reaction. I just try to share this reaction to what I love and want to share it. The pleasure is to give away what you love. If you do it just for yourself, it is not really creativity. Creativity, for me, is mostly something that can be shared and appreciated by others.

I do my best. It is not enough. Even in success, I am always surprised. I see too much of the weakness of my work. I am always surprised that many people don't care about the weakness. I have very few critics. The strongest critic comes from myself.

I am not so intellectual and complicated to give good answers. I do art simply because it is the only reaction I can have. I try to do it in the most positive way.

Godfrey Reggio—Filmmaker

A 1995 Heron Dance interview by Roderick MacIver

Godfrey Reggio is a filmmaker who lives and works in an old industrial building in Sante Fe. On the couch near his desk is a pile of pillows and blankets—that's where he sleeps. His films chronicle the destructive impact of the modern world on the environment and on the human psyche. His work includes the Qatsi Trilogy: Koyaanisqatsi, Powaqqatsi, *and* Naqoyqatsi. *I asked Reggio, "How would you define a life well lived?"*

First of all, I don't think we're here to be happy. Happiness is not something that can be sought. It is the result, the fruit of, the effect of. I believe that we're here to live creative lives. If we can't create our own condition of life, if we can't participate in that, if we can't use our energies at conjuring something that was within our spiritual imagination, within our poetic souls, which we all have—it's not limited to a few elite—then what's the point of being here? It's not to get a big house, get a car, have a vacation, have social security, punch in 9 to 5. To me, university diplomas can be death certificates. Diplomas often lead to the traditions of making a living, rather than creating a living.

I don't believe you can tell other people how to be happy, how to be creative, compassionate. It's only example that does that. If a teacher does anything, it is to provide an example that we can learn from.

A life of creativity is a life of risk. It is a life of going beyond your ordinary, of embracing the odyssey, of leaving your familiar, of trying to make a contribution. It could be through art, though I don't like that name. The word "art" has been hijacked by the Art Mafia. But, it could be through art, it could be through compassion, it could be through contemplation, it could be through devotion to someone or your children. It's something that is creative.

Who knows what causes a person to become inspired or what moves a person or what touches a person. We're metaphoric beings. We learn in terms of what we already know. We have to describe things in terms of the familiar.

Life goes by quickly, yet every moment we live is eternity as well. So, here we're dealing with these enormous paradoxes. I believe that it is through the creative act that one informs one's consciousness, and I've tried to live my life through act. Anything I know doesn't come from academia. It comes from experience.

To experience time and eternity beyond perception in our being, to me, is a thrill. I'm very happy to be here, even given the madness of the 20th century. I feel it's a privilege to have this breath of life. I feel it's a grace. To be more reflective on it, I guess I could. But somehow I don't think it's about me, I think it's about something all of us share. It's about this excitement for life if one can see beyond...

Once we see something, after a while it all looks normal. But if you stare at it, if you look at the ordinary in a way that you haven't seen it before, all of a sudden you start to see it in a luminous way. And I've tried to live my life that way. Not always successfully. And I've tried to make my films that way. Certainly not always successfully. But to try to see in the humility of the moment we're in, the dimensions that our mind, our senses, aren't even aware of.

To create one's own life is a risky business. There are no ground rules, but the road is full of mighty and heroic examples of men and women who have given their life over to creativity, who have not sought material gain, but who have sought gain in the realm of the spirit, which, for me, is what brings peacefulness or happiness to life.

Love is the fruit of beauty. When you see a beautiful tree, you fall in love—ah, beautiful flowers, the bluebells, the primroses—beauty enters the heart and creates love. That is why in the world today we lack love, because there is less and less beauty in our everyday lives. Whenever you make something with love, you feel humbled. You could not make such beautiful things on your own. It must come through divine inspiration. In that way, beauty and humility go together. It is an act of surrender to the divine source. The divine inspiration uses your body, your hands, and your talents, as a channel for beauty, whether it is a Henry Moore sculpture or a painting by Van Gogh or some beautiful peasant house in rural Vermont. Or beautiful shoes made in Rajistan... Therefore, beauty is a source of spiritual healing. For me, beauty is the essence of our being, the soul of our being.

- Satish Kumar, from
Issue 23 of HERON DANCE

Art is simply a result of expression during right feeling... Any material will do. After all, the object is not to make art, but to be in the wonderful state which makes art inevitable.

- Robert Henri, from
The Art Spirit

We each have a spiritual current that runs through our lives—a river. Connected to that current, our work, our life, has power. I constantly ask myself: What is my relationship to that current? Am I letting it guide me or am I forcing my will upon my life? It is so easy to lose touch with that current. When I am connected, my life has a flow. The most amazing things happen. Help comes my way, I meet "fellow-travelers," people whose energy supports mine, and we both come away reinforced. Doors open. Bills get paid. In a good month, I spend about a third of my time in that state of synchronicity.

When you turn your back on the current of your life, you are on your own. You are coming at life believing that you are strong enough, powerful enough on your own. The other way is to come at life from a place of humility.

Do I put living a spiritual life ahead of deadlines and achieving some tangible goal? Silence certainly plays a role. Being in touch with the spiritual current means first being able to listen to oneself, being in sync with oneself. You need silence to get there. Work of the spirit requires strength of spirit.

- Roderick MacIver, from
Issue 13 of HERON DANCE

The secret of the creative life is often to feel at ease with your own embarrassment. We are paid to take risks, to look silly. Some people like racing car drivers are paid to take risks in a more concrete way. We are paid to take risks in an emotional way.

- Paul Schraeder, interviewed on
"Fresh Air" on National Public Radio

Each morning we must hold out the chalice of our being to receive, to carry, and give back.

– Dag Hammarskjold

Chapter Four:

Offerings

He lived then, as he always had, with such inner fire that his life itself seemed worth while, book or no book. Traubel asked him the question once, "Suppose the whole damned thing went up in smoke, Walt: would you consider your life a failure?" He cried out at once with intense feeling: "Not a bit of it... No life is a failure. I have done the work: I have thrown my life into the work: ...my single simple life: putting it up for what it was worth: into the book—pouring it into the book: honestly, without stint, giving the book all, all, all: why should I call it a failure? Why? Why? I don't think a man can be so easily wrecked as that."

- Henry Seidel Canby,
Walt Whitman, An American

Neither a lofty degree
of intelligence nor imagination,
nor both together,
go to the making of a genius.
Love, love, love,
that is the soul of genius.

- Wolfgang Amadeus Mozart

The artist should have a powerful will. He should be powerful possessed by an idea. He should be intoxicated with the idea of the thing he wants to express. If his will is not strong he will see all kinds of unessential things. A picture should be the expression of the will of the painter.

- Robert Henri, from *The Art Spirit*

The creative act is a courageous, ancient gesture, a dynamic exploration of the dark mystery that is human existence. When I finally identified this face of creativity as sacred practice, I built a small alter in my studio and my work took on a depth of meaning it never had. Prayer and art suddenly meshed and became refined. It wasn't done in pursuit of holiness as I'd been taught in the child's corner of my life. Prayer became synonymous with art as authentic expression of my entire complex self.

- Adriana Diaz, from
The Soul of Creativity

I would like to believe that beauty is of deep import to our modern age. Without question, the intention of morality, philosophy, and religious belief is to bring hope, joy, peace, and freedom to mankind. But in our time, religion has lost its grip. Intellectualism has undermined spiritual aspiration in most people. At this juncture I would put the question: might not beauty, and the love of the beautiful, perhaps bring peace and harmony? Could it not carry us forward to new concepts of life's meaning? Would it not establish a fresh concept of nature? Would it not become a dove of peace between the various cultures of mankind?

- Soetsu Yanagi, from
The Unknown Craftsman

The sound of the sea, the curve of a horizon, wind in leaves, the cry of a bird leave manifold impressions in us. And suddenly, without our wishing it at all, one of these memories spills from us and finds expression in musical language… I want to sing my interior landscape with the simple artlessness of a child.

- Claude Debussy

We sat together at one summer's end,
That beautiful, mild woman, your close friend,
And you and I, and talked of poetry.
I said, "A line will take us hours maybe:
Yet if it does not seem a moment's thought,
Our stitching and unstitching has been naught.
- W. B. Yeats, *Adam's Curse*

Writing is hard work. A clear sentence is no accident.
Very few sentences come out right the first time,
or even the third time. Remember this as a consolation
in moments of despair. If you find that writing is hard,
it's because it is hard. It's one of the hardest things that people do.
- William Zinsser

The fine things we shall write if we have talent enough, are within us,
dimly, like the remembrance of a tune which charms though we cannot
recall its outline, or hum it, nor even sketch its metrical form, say
if there are pauses in it, or runs of rapid notes.
- Proust, *Return to the Present*

The modest domestic circumstances of Tolstoy, the lack of comfort in Rodin's rooms—it all points to the same thing: that one must make up one's mind: either this or that. Either happiness or art. On doit trouver le bonheur dam son art [one must find happiness in one's art]: that too, more or less, is what Rodin said. And it is all so clear, so clear. The great artists have all let their lives become overgrown like an old path and have borne everything in their art. Their lives have become atrophied, like an organ they no longer use.
- Rainer Maria Rilke in a letter to Clara Rilke, September 5, 1902

Greg Brown — Folksinger

HERON DANCE interview

It's something to sit and witness someone do what he loves. The whole audience gets beautifully lost when a performer sings from his heart. That's what folksinger Greg Brown does. Greg's music is important to me because he sings of the messy loveliness of life, with all its contradictions and confusions. As a character in his song "Rexroth's Daughter" says: "Life is like a thump-ripe melon. So sweet, and such a mess."

During my interview of him in 2003, I asked Greg if he felt any obligation to give voice to his political views:

No, I wouldn't say I do, because there're all kinds of music that can touch people and can be good and useful and healing in all kinds of ways. For example, I would say that a lot of jazz and blues music, which doesn't have any overt political message, promotes peace, 'cause music—good music that reaches people's souls—has the power to cross over all the lines we draw politically. So I think the responsibility of a musician or writer is to make music and write stories as honestly as he or she can. It's a big world, you know, and there's room for a lot of different approaches to this stuff. I think there just needs to be the intention to reach out. I feel an obligation to do that in my music.

Then I asked if he felt any obligation to have his music serve something greater.

Yeah, just lettin' it out, you know? And lettin' it out in a positive way, I guess. Very shortly after my father died, which was three years ago now, I felt like I received a very strong message from him. And the message was to use my writing and music the best I could on the positive side of things. And I am still trying to figure out exactly what he meant by that, because I know he didn't mean for me to write a bunch of Hallmark cards or something. I paid attention to that, and I think he was telling me something very important. But I know something: In these times we do have to pay attention. There's the love pile and the hate pile, is the way I look at it, and we've got to try and put as much stuff as we can in the love pile, however we can do that.

We shall not cease from exploration
And the end of all our exploring
Will be to arrive where we started
And know the place for the first time.
Through the unknown, remembered gate
When the last of earth left to discover
Is that which was the beginning;
At the source of the longest river
The voice of the hidden waterfall
And the children in the apple-tree
Not known, because not looked for
But heard, half-heard, in the stillness
Between two waves of the sea.

- T.S. Eliot, from
"Little Gidding" in Four Quartets

As a writer, I have to work with my imagination and my mind, and therefore I must lead a life that does not take my imagination away from my work—which means that I must go away from people at times. I find that the most important part of working is not the period when I am actually writing, but the periods when I stop writing between one day and the next morning. That period is terribly important and, though I cannot write in it, it is one in which my imagination should not be caught up in other things since it is an instrument of my writing. That is the sort of incubation period, a time of vulnerable growth. Something goes on, and then I like to go on long walks in the country just by myself. I would love to write twenty-four hours a day, but words are so exacting, such hard work, that I cannot do more than three or, if I am lucky, four hours at a time, however much I long to push on. So, in between, I am anxious to get on to the next morning; I can hardly wait to get back to it.

- Laurens van der Post, from
Walk with a White Bushman

Tom Wisner – Folksinger

HERON DANCE interview by Roderick MacIver

Tom is a poet, folk musician, and disciple of the waters of Chesapeake. He is 76 years old and has been connected to the river all his life—first as a boy growing up on the James and Potomac Rivers—Chesapeake tributaries. As an adult, he became an outreach instructor for the Chesapeake Biological Laboratory. For the last 20 years, he has been a poet, storyteller, and folksinger, traveling around the area, mostly to local schools. We had been talking about the role of beauty in our lives when he said:

The songs are, for me, a source of peace, creating a sense of unity, and connection with the flow of things. If that is beauty, I could talk about that. I could talk about the peace that comes to me in that. That is what my songs have taught me. A lot about rhythm, pace. That is what they do for me. I don't go through a day without song. It brings the process of being with others into another form.

Then Tom sang:

I'm made of water, flowin' water
Sun and salts and winds that blow
Winds that blow.
Though my bones were
Formed in the mountains
It's through my blood
This river flows.

Drivin' down, the wind will sound
The rain will fall and roll on by.
Lord, I am mighty grateful for
Love I see in my brother's eye.
And for the mighty river bringin'
Life a rollin' from the sky

I love that song so much. It amazes me that I wrote it. I keep returnin' to it. These songs teach me. Do you feel that? There is a learning in that that is beyond the writing or the picturing. It is a learning that is deep and rhythmic.

I don't know why I love water so much.

To be a good writer, you not only have to write a great deal, but you have to care. You do not have to have a complicated moral philosophy. But a writer always tries, I think, to be a part of the solution, to understand a little about life, and to pass this on. Even someone as grim and unsentimental as Samuel Beckett, with his lunatics in garbage cans or up to their necks in sand, whose lives consist of pawing through the contents of their purses, stopping to marvel at each item, gives us great insight into what is true, into what helps. He gets it right—that we're born astride the grave and that this planet can feel as cold and uninhabitable as the moon—and he knows how to make it funny. He smiles an oblique and private smile at us, the most delicious smile of all, and this changes how we look at life. A few small things seem suddenly clear, things to which we can cling, and this makes us feel like part of the solution. (But perhaps we have the same problem with the word *solution* as we do with the word *moral*. It sounds so fixative, and maybe we have gone beyond fixing. Maybe all we can do is to make our remaining time here full of gentleness and good humor.)

- Anne Lamott, from *Bird by Bird*

Or you could be the one who takes the long way home
Roll down your window, turn off your phone
See your life as a gift from the great unknown
And your task is to receive it
Tell your kid a story, hold your lover tight
Make a joyful noise, swim naked at night
Read a poem a day, call in well sometimes and
Laugh when they believe it

- Mary Chapin Carpenter, from
her song "The Long Way Home"

The proper use of imagination is to give beauty to the world... The gift of imagination is used to cast over the commonplace workaday world a veil of beauty and make it throb with our esthetic enjoyment.

- Lin Yü-T'ang

Art is both love and friendship, and understanding; the desire to give. It is not charity, which is the giving of things, it is more than kindness, which is the giving of self. It is both the taking and giving of beauty, the turning out to the light of the inner folds of awareness of the spirit. It is the recreation on another plane of the realities of the world; the tragic and wonderful realities of earth and men, and of all the inner relations of these.

- Ansel Adams in a letter to Cedric Wright, June 10, 1937

Chapter Five:

The Creative Spirit as a Beacon

...a work of art opens a void, a moment of silence, a question without an answer, provokes a breach without reconciliation where the world is forced to question itself.

- Michel Foucault

If I were inclined to have my work do anything at all, I would want for it to turn the reader back upon himself, to provoke him to examine himself. I am, however, not inclined to think that way.

I am trying very selfishly to find out something about Harry Crews—I write because I don't understand or know myself, and not understanding or knowing myself is, among other things, very frightening. I do know that I am capable of bestial behavior, and I know that I am capable of rank cruelty—emotional cruelty and blood cruelty, too. And the more I can understand about that, the more I can live with it.

The poet Yevushenko said that the most beautiful, aching work in the world is to be yourself. I suppose I write in order to live—in the best sense of that word—to find out what I am. That's a rambling, unsatisfying answer, but out of that kind of mulligan stew of fault and emotional reaction you make stuff. Out of that, you try to make something firm and beautiful and clean and sharp and focused and memorable and compelling.

- Erik Bledsoe, *Getting Naked with Harry Crews* (Interviews)

And the other thing is I think you do it as a debt of honor—if you've got that creative voice inside of you that has something to communicate, that just longs to tell its version of things or to entertain or to inspire or to try to be a part of the solution or just to be heard—you know, to stop being a person who is silenced—then I think you have to honor that or you're just doomed.

- Anne Lamott

What is your truth? Ask your heart, your back, your bones, and your dreams. Listen to that truth with your whole body. Understand that this truth will destroy no one and that you're too old to be sent to your room.

Move into your truth as though it were an old house. Walk through each room. See, hear, and feel what it is to live there. Try to love what you find, and remember the words that come to you as you explore.

If you embrace it, if you are faithful to it, your truth will reward you with unimaginable freedom and intimacy with yourself and others. You won't land in a world made to order; some people in your life may not like what you write. But those who remain will be allies, people who breathe deeply and listen. It will feel good to be seen completely and loved as you are. As Natalie Goldberg said after her friend found and read a piece of work-in-progress that she had left out from the day's writing, "I feel good because I don't care that she sees how I really am. I'm glad. I want someone to know me."

- John Lee,
from *Writing from the Body*

Do not let the fact that things are not made for you, that conditions are not as they should be, stop you. Go on anyway. Everything depends on those who go on anyway.

- Robert Henri, from *The Art Spirit*

I think visual art and music creates a universal type of expression that anyone can respond to. I think artists need to keep inventing new forms of expression. What comes at people from the popular culture is so intense. I feel its our obligation to invent art forms that are more and more available to the people. It does nothing to complain that no one's going to the gallery to see your painting. "Those darn people, why aren't they coming in here and looking at my painting?" Artists should be asking themselves instead, "How can I use the internet? What about video? What about mixing mediums?" We have to reach out to people.

- Pamela Timmins, from
Issue 51 of Heron Dance

But I must work on in full calmness and serenity... The world concerns me only in so far as I feel a certain debt and duty towards it, because I have walked on the earth for thirty years, and out of gratitude want to leave some souvenir in the shape of drawings or pictures, not made to please a certain tendency in art, but to express a sincere human feeling. So this work is the aim—and through concentration upon that one idea, everything one does is simplified. Now the work goes slowly—a reason the more to lose no time.

- Vincent Van Gogh,
from a letter to his brother Theo

Chapter Six: *Fuel for the Fire*

Nobody grasped you by the shoulder while there was still time. Now the clay of which you were shaped has dried and hardened and naught in you will ever awaken the sleeping musician, the poet, the astronomer that possibly inhabited you in the beginning.

- Antoine de Saint Exupery from *Wind, Sand and Stars*

His daddy financed him. Miles Davis always had backup. He knew he could go out there and do these things because his Daddy was there. Doctor Davis was there for him. That is very important. His father was the one who told him, "Don't go out there and sound like a mockingbird. A mockingbird is copying. Sound like yourself. Sound like Miles. Play Miles."

- Quincy Troupe, from *The Miles Davis Radio Project.*

Sometimes when I was starting a new story and I could not get it going, I would sit in front of the fire and squeeze the peel of the little oranges into the edge of the flame and watch the sputter of blue that they made. I would stand and look out over the roofs of Paris and think, "Do not worry. You have always written before and you will write now. All you have to do is write one true sentence. Write the truest sentence that you know." So finally I would write one true sentence and then go on from there.

I learned not to think about anything that I was writing from the time I stopped writing until I started again the next day. That way my subconscious would be working on it and at the same time I would be listening to other people and noticing everything, I hoped; learning, I hoped; and I would read so that I would not think about my work and make myself impotent to do it.

- Ernest Hemingway from *A Moveable Feast*

Could Hamlet have been written by a committee, or the Mona Lisa painted by a club? Could the New Testament have been composed as a conference report? Creative ideas do not spring from groups. They spring from individuals. The divine spark leaps from the finger of God to the finger of Adam, whether it takes the ultimate shape in a law of physics or a law of the land, a poem or a policy, a sonata or a mechanical composition.

- A. Whitney Griswold

I am unable to distinguish between the feeling I have for life and my way of expressing it.
- Henry Matisse

Poets may be delightful creatures in the meadow or the garret, but they are menaces on the assembly line.
- Rollo May, *The Courage To Create*

I work every day. I don't care whether I know what's coming or not. I work. At least I sit at the typewriter. I tell myself, "You go sit there three hours. You don't have to write anything. Just sit there." So pretty soon you write something, just try something; and you find your way out. But sometimes it's bad, and you know it's bad. When that happens, at least me, I get really down on myself. I begin to doubt everything. I think, "Hell, you weren't a writer to start with. Now you've got this charade. You really ought to . . ." I just say terrible things to myself. Then, voila, I go to school.

I like to teach, see. That's the weird thing about it. I really do. I enjoy it. The students, they're honest, they'll run you up a tree. They won't take much phony stuff. I go in there and teach a sensational class. Just get in there and just wing and talk and get 'em excited and get all... When I come out of the class, I think, "Well, buddy, you might can't write, but goddamn, you sure can teach."

I've sort of got a theory in my head about that. I think every man ought to have more than one thing he does well. He doesn't have to get his bread by it, but if he's just really a good, competent, fine, amateur butterfly preserver or coin-collector or Sunday painter or bicycle rider or anything, so that he can go out there and get his head clean...

You see, I don't think of writing as a job. I think of it as a...almost like an avocation. I would be writing novels if nobody was publishing them. I'd write novels if I had to send them out to sea in a bottle... The hardest thing for me is to control my personal life so I can do the amount of work I want to do. I need to work. I have guilt feelings if I don't work, sourceless anxiety.
- Erik Bledsoe, *Getting Naked with Harry Crews* (Interviews)

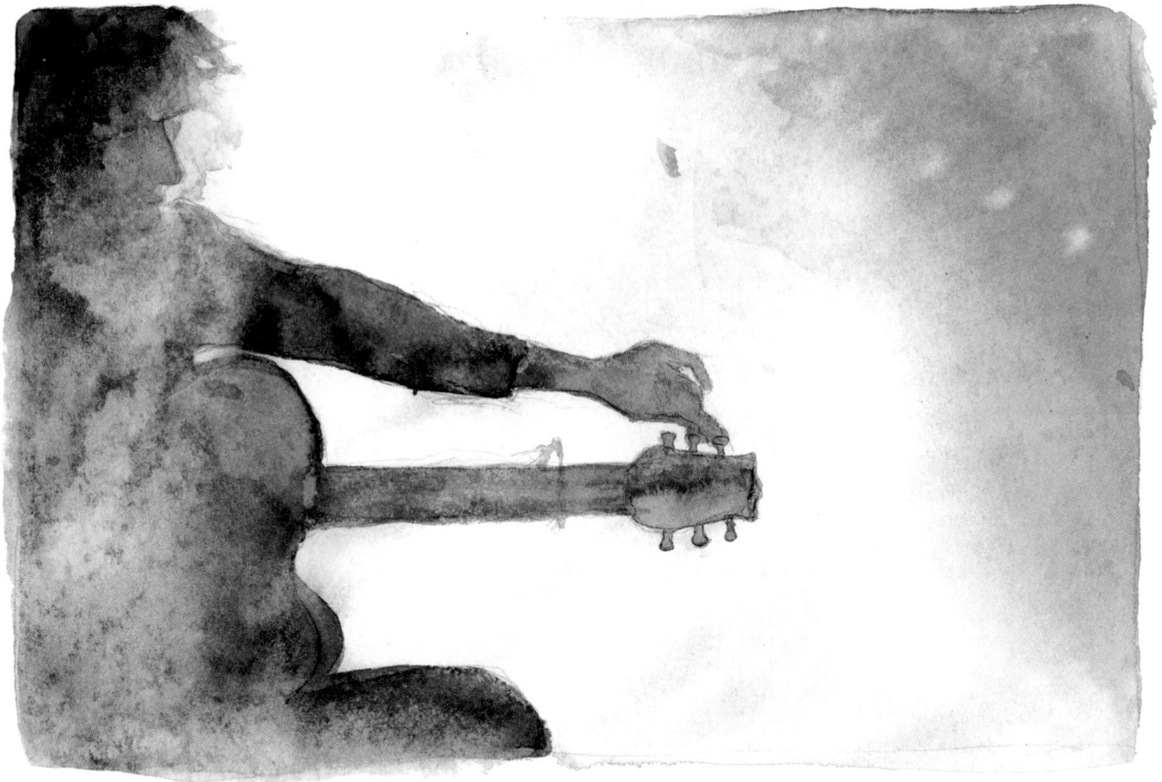

Chris Smither — Folksinger

I interviewed Chris Smither, one of my favorite songwriter/singers for Issue 42 of HERON DANCE. *Chris Smither—a soft spoken, warm, thoughtful man—has been singing on the road and making albums for 37 years. He's seen some hard times. I asked him to share what beliefs he's carried with him since he was young and to describe how they have served him during his 58 years.*

There were beliefs that I had to get rid of that were really harmful, like the illusion that you can be independent. People take pride in being independent. But the idea that dependence is to be avoided, and self-sufficiency exalted, is so counterproductive. I mean, there is nothing on Earth that is independent. We are all interdependent. You cannot get away from it. The sooner you recognize that fact, the happier you will be.

Then I asked him if he felt any obligation towards his gift.

Yes, I do. I've been singin' and songwritin' for a livin' for 37 years—longer than that if you count when I first picked up a ukulele. There was a turning point ten years ago where the whole thrust of what I was doing, and the way I thought about it, changed entirely. I remember this specific instance. Twenty-seven years of playing music for a living built up to this one moment.

I was at a festival in Canada. It was a big event

and I was feeling cheated because I had been promised a spot on the main stage and didn't get it. I had been led to believe that I would get at least 20 minutes of my own, you know? But instead, they sort of loosely collected everybody who did anything that remotely resembled blues and put 'em all up on the stage together. There were four solo acoustic artists and one band up there together. Of course, the band sort of overshadowed everybody, you know? The whole thing wasn't very well thought out. I was annoyed. They wanted us to just jam together on all these songs—one after another. It was irritating. What if you put Brahms and Beethoven and Bach all together? Would you just say, "Well, they're all piano players. They can jam. They can play together?" No!

It came my turn. I played the song. There were ten to fifteen thousand people out there—a big deal for me! After I played my song, the others had their turns. As it went further down the line, and I was just waitin' for my turn to come around again, inside I was just seething. I thought, "This is so unfair!"

But a change came in the time that it took for my turn to come around again. It suddenly dawned on me, and I don't know how this happened. It was like a little window opening someplace in my brain. I guess it was the culmination of a lot of lessons that I've been learning over the years. And I said to myself,

"You know what? This isn't about me. This is about music. This is about the music! And the only thing that I have to do is play the song, just lay the song out the best way I know how. And what happens to it after that is beyond my control. It has always been beyond my control. I'll never be able to make it happen. There are all these little conditions that I'll never be able to touch. The only thing that I can control is what I do and my attitude towards it. That's it. And as long as I keep thinkin' that this is about me, I'm gonna be unhappy. And as soon as I think that it's all about the song itself, and what happens to the song, the better off I'll be."

So, it came around my turn, and I played the song, and I played the song in that state of mind. Of course, it would be very nice to be able to say that the crowd was blown away and cheered me to the sky, but that didn't happen. But I felt so much better about it. That was the whole thing.

There is a service to the gift itself, you see? You have to serve it. It does not serve you.

And in terms of an obligation to it, I'm not sure that I feel necessarily an obligation to the gift. It's just part of me, you know? It's just part of what I do, and I feel enormously lucky that I'm allowed to make a living doing that.

And, of course, all of this is very different from the way it was when I first started. When I first started, when I was a kid, I was just like every other kid. I had dreams of super stardom. I was going to be a household word, and all the women in the world were gonna love me. I went through a really long period of just totally self-destructive behavior and wound up very sick from alcohol abuse and, to a certain extent, drug abuse. But the main drug was alcohol. And it was really getting out of that that taught me almost everything that I know about how to rearrange my priorities and the way I think about things. Because there's nothin', nothin' more self-centered than an addict. It's what makes the affliction what it is, the need to sustain self, in spite of anything else that might be going on around you.

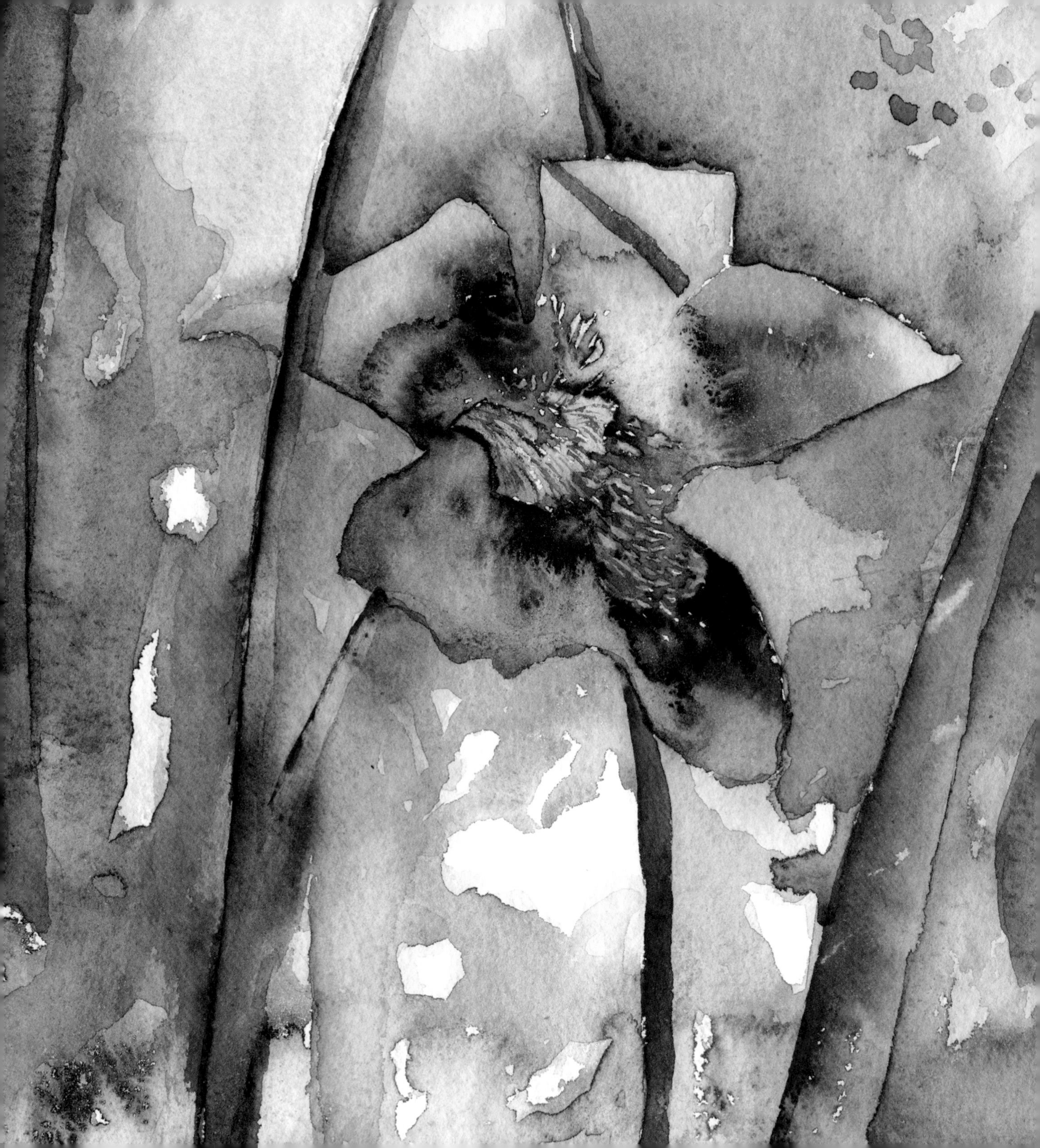

Carel Pieter Brest van Kempen – Artist

HERON DANCE interview by Roderick MacIver

In Issue 23 of HERON DANCE, *I interviewed Carel Pieter Brest van Kempen, an artist in Salt Lake City. His responses to my questions were unusually careful and thoughtful; his home is simply and aesthetically furnished with sunny, open rooms. In the driveway were parked two vans—one is a mini-van, the other is older and larger. It turned out that in order to stay with his art, he lived in the van and its predecessor, an older, more dilapidated van that was ultimately impounded. As his art gained recognition, he moved into a basement apartment and then was able to buy the house where we met.*

He started the interview by stating that art was at the borders of his understanding. "Thank God, words are not my medium," he said. "I would definitely still be living in my van. I see myself as a naturalist who paints, rather than an artist who is interested in nature. Most of what I try to do is to describe my view of nature—something I have grappled with all my life.

I asked Carel about the circumstances leading up to his homelessness.

I used to have no discipline, no attention span. And no patience. From the time I was eighteen, I worked in restaurants, on construction, or bartending. I tried to do art at the same time, but not very successfully. I couldn't focus. Until ten years ago. When I turned thirty I realized that I was doing exactly what I was doing when I turned twenty. That was kind of a shock. Actually, it was a shock to see that I had actually lived that long. I subconsciously suspected that I wouldn't. I was kind of reckless.

I made an active effort, starting in the winter of 1988, to really try to make a living as an artist. By 1992, I either had to get a job or move into my van. I decided on the van. It actually turned out to be a relief—the threat of being homeless had been hanging over my head for so long. It was nice not having to worry about it anymore. Worrying about it was a lot worse than actually being it.

I asked Carel if he considered getting a job and painting at night—or even a part-time job.

I decided that if I really wanted to do art, I had to completely focus on it. And I had no distractions in the van. I didn't have to think about anything. I had pretty much no social life because people didn't want to be around me. I had no money. I looked shabby. I usually tried to keep myself fairly clean, but it is hard to keep yourself really clean living in a van... It was good for me as a person. It was good to focus, to be completely unconcerned with putting on the façade, with putting on airs, with dealing with people. It was healthy to drop off the planet and be in a meditative state for a couple of years—which I think painting is when it is going right. That is what I strive for. When I am working, I pretty much enter the world I am creating.

My art developed rapidly. When I moved into my van, my stuff was good enough to get into shows, but it wasn't good enough to excel. It was during the time in the van that I went from being adequate to being good.

I am compelled. I work about ten hours a day—which is a lot less than I used to—seven days a week. Unless I am traveling. I am putting off taking down time. I spent my twenties in downtime...

I asked Carel if he ever considered giving up.

No, I never did. I never did. Not completely. I had negative thoughts that were a small part of my consciousness but I never really felt like giving up. I always felt I could do it.

The Ten Commandments on Seeing/Drawing

1. You shall draw everything and every day.
2. You shall not wait for inspiration, for it comes not while you wait, but while you work.
3. You shall not forget all you think you know and even more, all you have been taught.
4. You shall not adore your good drawings and promptly forget your bad ones.
5. You shall not draw with exhibitions in mind, nor to please any critic but yourself.
6. You shall trust none but your own eye and make your hand follow it.
7. You shall consider the mouse you draw as more important than the contents of all of the museums in the world, for
8. You shall love the ten thousand things with all your heart and a blade of grass as yourself.
9. Let each drawing be your first: A celebration of the eye awakened.
10. You shall not worry about "being of your time" for you are your time and it is brief.

- Frederick Franck,
from *The Awakened Eye*

An artist must have downtime, time to do nothing. Defending our right to such time takes courage, conviction, and resiliency. Such time, space, and quiet will strike our family as a withdrawal from them. It is… An artist requires the upkeep of creative solitude. An artist requires the time of healing alone. Without this period of recharging, our artist becomes depleted… We strive to be good, to be nice, to be helpful, to be unselfish. We want to be generous, of service, of the world. But what we really want is to be left alone. When we can't get others to leave us alone, we eventually abandon ourselves. To others, we may look like we're there. We may act like we're there. But our true self has gone to ground. Over time, it becomes something worse than out of sorts. Death threats are issued.

- Julia Cameron, from
The Artist's Way

What would it be like if you lived each day, each breath, as a work of art in progress? Imagine that you are a masterpiece unfolding every second of every day, a work of art taking form with every breath.

- Thomas Crum, from
www.thomascrum.com

Making Your Living From Creative Work

A point of view is necessarily subjective, but its authenticity depends on objectivity, and objectivity demands an honesty sooner or later painful. I look for the rare artists who have had the resolution, the courage and the pertinacity to observe, examine and reexamine on its own terms the given range of their singularity until the particular yields the universal.

- Anne Truitt, from *Prospect*

The work of an art student is no light matter. Few have the courage and stamina to see it through.

- Robert Henri, *The Art Spirit*

It's very possible that your life in art—your successful life in art—might be a struggle from start to finish.

- Sally Warner

I have been doing this kind of composing…for most of my life. I know that familiar river is there, the river of vowels with its rocky bed of consonants, and I know that any stimulus at all will find related stuff that comes floating down the stream.

- Robert Pinsky, Poet

It is a fact that no one ever made a wood engraving or wrote a sestina by merely being creative. That's like a tail wagging a dog, for God's sake. Rather than teaching kids to be "creative" they should be taught what art really is. They should be taught the history of its practitioners, and a good deal about the role craftsmanship plays in the process. They should be taught form, not finger paints. They should be taught that art, contrary to the conventional wisdom, is not self-indulgent. They should be taught that art does not come to those who wait. They should be taught that art comes from those who do—that the very genius of art lies in action. In doing. They should be taught that art comes from study and from hard work and from solid craftsmanship, they should know that beyond determination and persistence, art comes about only through study, work, and knowledge of their craft.

I taught school for twenty-five years. I have no record of how many students I taught over all those years, but it has to be in the tens of hundreds. Based on that experience I can say honestly that I never met a student who was not "creative," nor did I ever meet one who was not "talented." A few of those students are now professional graphic designers, painters, architects, potters, and furniture makers. But why them and not the others, if, as I say, all of them were creative and talented?

The answer is simple: some of my students persisted and some did not. Those who did not persist were the ones lacking sufficient interest, drive, and discipline. Those who did persist persisted because they had energy, they had courage (or "sand" as my granddaddy would have put it), and they developed a need to work.

Moser's three rules for the so-called creative life, are, therefore,

Persistence
Indefatigable energy
The habit of work

- *In the Face of Presumption, Essays, Speeches & Incidental Writings* by Barry Moser

You write with ease to show your breeding,
But easy writing's curst hard reading.
- R. B. Sheridan

A writer is someone for whom writing is more difficult
than it is for other people.
- Thomas Mann

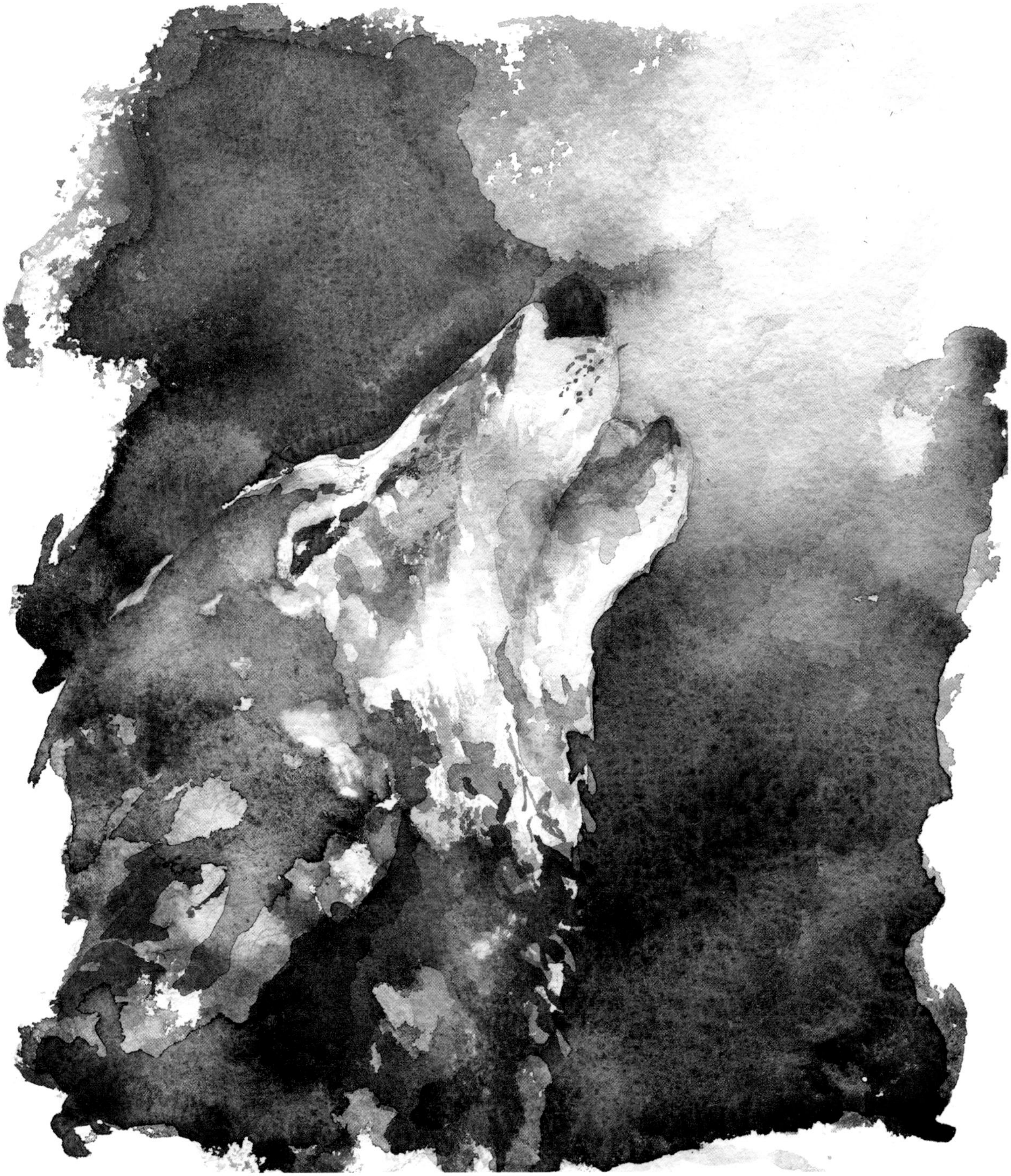

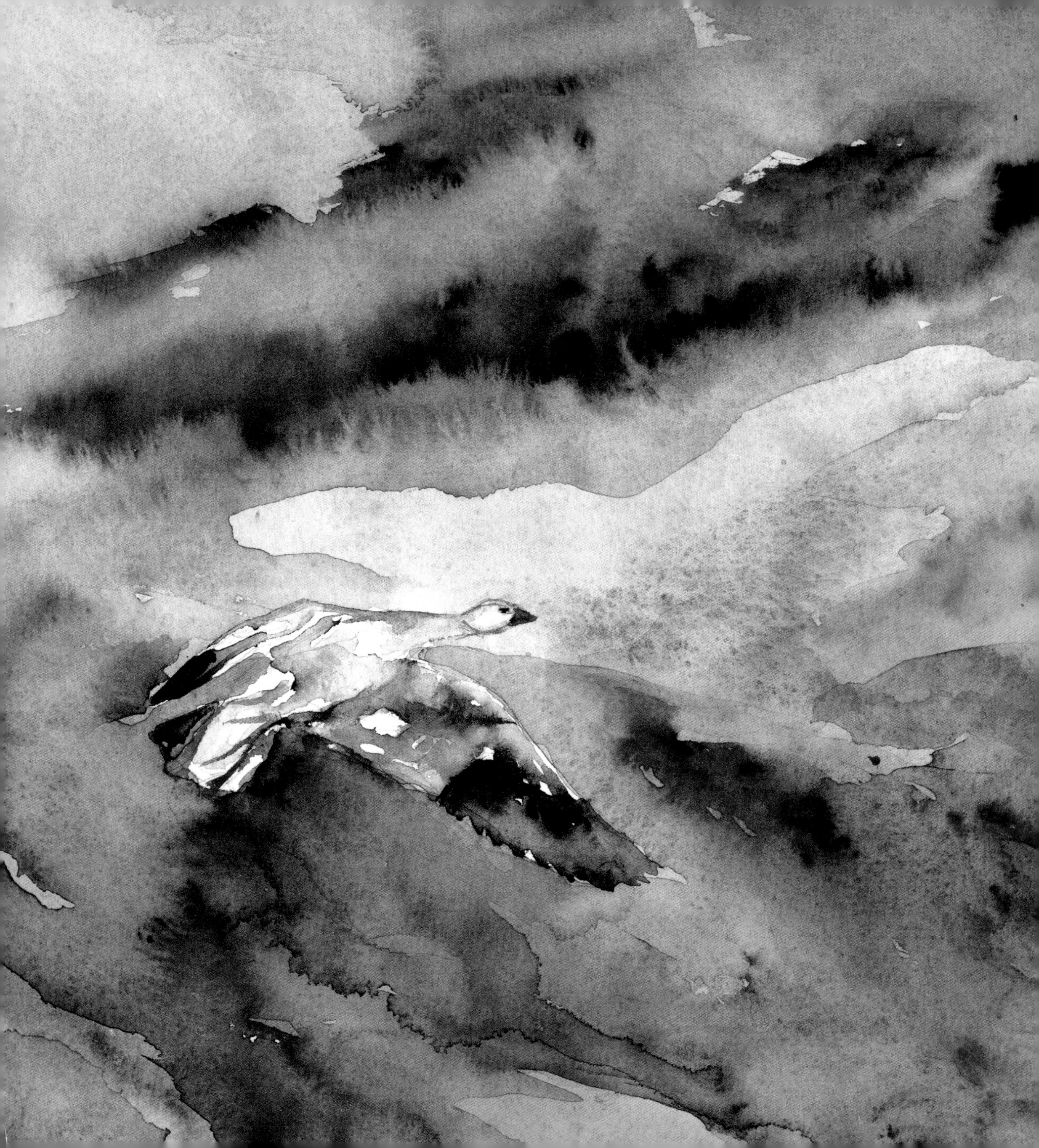

Talent. Ahhhhh, everyone talks about talent. Talent helps. Listen, get all the talent you can. But writing is guts and it's courage. You cannot have a failure of courage. Everybody in the world is telling you you're no good, and you can't do it, and it's not going to work. You've got to keep talking to yourself, say, "Come on, son. Come on..."

If you look at any writers, if you really look at them, what you see is a trail of mucus and blood and guts and everything else. I hink that every writer of any consequence or a writer that tries to be of consequence and write something of merit, that costs him an awful, awful lot. If you're married, what you give to the typewriter, you can't give to the girl. That may be all right for a year or two. It may be all right for eighteen years. But sooner or later, it's going to catch up with things. While fathers are out teaching their sons to fly-fish, you're trying to teach yourself how to do something with your craft. If you're a person of feeling, if you feel things keenly and deeply—and I don't think you can be a writer unless you feel things not just for the moment but they live in you—that costs you. I don't think you can be a writer of consequence and merit unless you have grave doubts about yourself, about what you've done and who you are and whom you've hurt. And that costs you. And so, it all costs you. What is left is what all of us are going to get, a chance to know what it's like to die.

- Erik Bledsoe, *Getting Naked with Harry Crews* (Interviews)

The following excerpts are from a HERON DANCE interview (Issue 35) of Fritz Hull, founder of the Whidbey Institute. We were talking about the challenges of sticking with your calling during the tough times:

Staying with our bliss, our calling, over the long haul has in fact brought me and Vivian our happiness. And that means staying with it in times of unhappiness. Riding out the storms, the times of bewilderment, and hanging on and staying with it. Coming through those periods, there is a confirmation, and that inner confirmation brings the happiness that makes it all feel worthwhile. There is a great line from Annie Dillard which I love. She says, "The thing is to stalk your calling in a certain skilled and supple way. To locate the most tender and live spot, and plug into that pulse." Isn't that great? It is from the story of the weasel.

To me it comes from Spirit. It comes from relationship with the mystery. What makes our heart sing? Where do we find that lilt in our hearts? What makes us crotchety? What nourishes us? What makes us smile? What makes us thankful?

When you stay with it and move through the seasons, you learn spring follows winter. It will happen. And it will probably happen in a way that you will have forgotten how beautiful it is. It is happening right now in these woods. We need to allow things the time to come into their own. To their moment of flowering, of opportunity, and to be there and intersect that opportunity, to be taken and lifted by that opportunity onto the next one, which will then include the next dark time. Probably. No doubt. There will be more bewilderment.

It requires a surrender to the call. And the call is both graceful and demanding. It requires wholeheartedness. That is the key. It is the opposite of an energy leakage, of things drifting off or being bleached away or being stolen from you. Energy leakage is the opposite of wholeheartedness. It is whatever drags me down and sideways and steals my energy. It steals my devotion. Devotion is wholeheartedness.

She painted rapidly yet meticulously, pausing only to eat, and usually she was finished with a small canvas by the time the daylight faded. Those were her best days. When a canvas was very large, however, and took longer than a day to paint, she seldom saw anyone or went anywhere until it was done, turning it to the wall if the housekeeper or anyone else entered her studio. Or, if she was dissatisfied with the result, she stubbornly worked off and on for months, painting the same canvass over and over-even though she knew that it was probably useless because her best pictures were usually those she painted the fastest.

- Laurie Lisle from *Portrait of an Artist* (about Georgia O'Keefe)

I was not an overnight success, even after I sold the strip. Peanuts did not take the world by storm immediately. It was a long grind. It took Peanuts about four years to attract nationwide attention, but it took ten years to become really entrenched.

- Charles Shulz

Research done by my colleague John R. Hayes and I indicates that nobody reaches world class in less than ten years of diligent application. Bobby Fischer became a chess grand master in slightly less than ten years. It took a bit more than ten years for Mozart. Mozart was a slow learner.

- Nobel Laureate Herbert A. Simon, from a 1985 lecture.

Nobody worked harder than Mozart. By the time he was twenty-eight years old, his hands were deformed because of all the hours he had spent practicing, performing, and gripping a quill pen to compose. That's the missing element in the popular portrait of Mozart. Certainly, he had a gift that set him apart from others. He was the most complete musician imaginable, one who wrote for all instruments in all combinations, and no one has written greater music for the human voice. Still, few people, even those hugely gifted, are capable of the application and focus that Mozart displayed throughout his short life. As Mozart himself wrote to a friend, "People err who think my art comes easily to me. I assure you, dear friend, nobody has devoted so much time and thought to composition as I. There is not a famous master whose music I have not industriously studied through many times."

- Twyla Tharp from *The Creative Habit*

There are no easy ruts to get into which lead to happiness.

- Robert Henri, *The Art Spirit*

The object in life is to find that undertaking, that occupation with which you have infinite patience.

- John Ruskin

Writing is a form of therapy; sometimes I wonder how all those who do not write, compose or paint can manage to escape the madness, the melancholia, the panic fear which is inherent in the human situation.

- Graham Greene

I was always willing to undergo hardship or whatever it took to be able to stay with my work. I could have quit many times—given up, because it is no great art in life to be poor and hungry, and that's what I was.

I lose my confidence sometimes, and that's where the courage part comes in. I'm only halfway self-confident... If you have determination, you're going to use that determination to take the place of confidence.

- Erskine Caldwell

Isaac Asimov received numerous rejections before his first acceptance of one of his science-fiction stories. But even though Asimov says those rejections bruised his ego, he had enough confidence in his ability to keep trying. "I was always pretty sure that eventually I would sell. It was just a matter of how long I would have to wait."

- Isaac Asimov as quoted in the book, *The Achievement Factors* by B. Eugene Griessman

Recommended Books on Watercolor and Creativity

1. *The Art Spirit* by Robert Henri
   "Explores in a very thought-provoking way the motivation behind art and artists."

2. *Painting People in Watercolor: A Design Approach* by Alex Powers
   "Amazing facility for design."

3. *Charles Reid's Watercolor Secrets* by Charles Reid
   "Reid's new book (see 1 above)."

4. *An American in Paris* by LeRoy Neiman
   "Wonderful use of form and color."

5. *Trevor Chamberlain: A Personal View—Light and Atmosphere in Watercolour* by Trevor Chamberlain
   "Master of watercolor technique."

6. *The Natural Way to Paint: Rendering the Figure in Watercolor Simply and Beautifully* by Charles Reid
   "I am inspired by Charles Reid's relaxed watercolor technique."

7. *In the Face of Presumptions: Essays, Speeches & Incidental Writings* by Barry Moser
   "A master of several art forms, including watercolor, describes the role of persistence in the making of an artist."

8. *The Creative Habit: Learn It and Use It for Life* by Twyla Tharp
   "MacArthur Award winner, choreographer, also describes the artist's life and its relationship to discipline and hard work."

9. *The Creative Artist: A Fine Artist's Guide to Expanding Your Creativity and Achieving Your Artistic Potential* by Nita Leland
   "Leland's selection of art inspires me."

10. *Artist's Manual: A Complete Guide to Painting and Drawing Materials and Techniques* edited by Angela Gair
    "As with the previous book, I like the selection of paintings."

11. *Drawing on the Right Side of the Brain* by Betty Edwards
    "I have not looked at this book in years, but I found it really helpful when I got serious about drawing."

12. *Writing Down the Bones* by Natalie Goldberg
"This is the book that gives us permission to let our hair down. Freeing."

13. *Writing from the Body* by John Lee with Ceci Miller-Kritsberg
"The subtitle says it all: For writers, artists and dreamers who want to free their voice."

14. *On Writing: A Memoir of the Craft* by Stephen King
"An inspiring and entertaining book about his life and his craft."

15. *Bird by Bird: Some Instructions on Writing and Life* by Anne Lamott
"My other favorite book on the writer's life."

16. *The Creative Habit: Learn it and Use it for Life* by Twyla Tharp
"Twyla is a creative powerhouse who shares her gifts generously. Very useful."

17. *Artist's Way: A Spiritual Path to Higher Creativity* by Julia Cameron
"This book has helped countless people discover their creativity."

18. *Uncommon Genius: Tracing the Creative Impulse with Forty Winners of the MacArthur Award* by Denise Shekerjian
"Shekerjianoffers us a fascinating look at genius through her interviews with MacArthur Award winners."

19. *Simple Abundance: A Daybook of Comfort and Joy* by Sarah Ban Breathnach
"This book guided me towards a creative life by teaching me how to nourish myself."

20. *Zen and the Art of Making a Living: A Practical Guide to Creative Career Design* by Laurence G. Boldt
"An important book for anyone who is trying to follow their passion."

List of Illustrations

All the watercolors in this book are by Roderick MacIver, founder of HERON DANCE. Select watercolors from this list are available as full-color, limited-edition prints on the HERON DANCE Web site (www.herondance.org) by typing the title in the search bar. If you have trouble finding the image you would like or do not have access to the internet, please call HERON DANCE toll free at 888-304-3766 or send an email to heron@herondance.org. Thank you.

** Also available as a notecard.*

HERON DANCE Press & Art Studio is a nonprofit 501(c)(3) organization founded in 1995.

HERON DANCE explores the beauty and mystery of the natural world through art and words. It is a work of love, an effort to produce something that is thought-provoking and beautiful. We offer A Pause for Beauty, The HERON DANCE Nature Art Journal, and notecards, books, and calendars.

We invite you to visit us at www.herondance.org to view the hundreds of watercolors by Roderick MacIver and to browse the hundreds of pages of book excerpts, poetry, essays, and interviews of authors and artists.

Nonprofit Donations

HERON DANCE donates thousands of notecards and the use of hundreds of images to small nonprofits every year. We also donate books and prints for fundraisers. Please contact us for more information.

The HERON DANCE Nature Art Journal

Available by subscription, The HERON DANCE Nature Art Journal is a 72-page full-color journal published twice a year that features nature watercolors by Roderick MacIver throughout. In its latest incarnation, it is a semi-fictional account of a wild artist who loves wild places, wild rivers, and wild women. It is a celebration of the gift of life! Visit our Web site to get more information (click Subscribe or Renew, then Plans for the HERON DANCE Nature Art Journal) or to sign up.

Our Free Weekly E-newsletter: A Pause for Beauty

Each issue features a new watercolor or acrylic ink painting, and a poem, quotation, or reflection. Over 25,000 people have signed up for A Pause for Beauty. To sign up or view our archives, visit our website.

Watercolors by Roderick MacIver

Hundreds of nature watercolors are available as signed limited-edition prints and originals at www.herondance.org.

Online Gallery

We offer notecards, daybooks, calendars, address books, and blank journals that feature Roderick MacIver watercolors, along with inspirational titles from HERON DANCE Press, including *The Heron Dance Book of Love and Gratitude*.

HERON DANCE *Community*

The HERON DANCE community consists of over 12,000 subscribers to our print journal and over 25,000 readers of our free daily e-mail A Pause for Beauty. To connect with other Heron Dancers, please visit our Facebook page. Links to that page and to founder Rod MacIver's page can be found by going to the HERON DANCE Web site, then clicking About Heron Dance and then Connect with Other Heron Dancers.

全彩
少儿版

思维导图

Mind Maps® for Kids

Max Your Memory and Concentration

记忆力与专注力训练

（英）东尼·博赞◎著　刘艳◎译

化学工业出版社
·北京·

图书在版编目（CIP）数据

思维导图 (全彩少儿版)：记忆力与专注力训练 / (英) 东尼·博赞 (Tony Buzan) 著；刘艳译 .
—北京：化学工业出版社，2018.2（2018.5 重印）
思维导图（全彩少儿版）
书名原文 :Mind Maps for Kids: Max Your Memory and Concentration
ISBN 978-7-122-30737-8

Ⅰ .①思… Ⅱ .①东… ②刘… Ⅲ .①记忆能力—能力培养—少儿读物 ②思维训练—少儿读物 Ⅳ .① B842.3-49 ② B80-49

中国版本图书馆 CIP 数据核字（2017）第 247100 号

Mind Maps for Kids: Max Your Memory and Concentration，1st edition by Tony Buzan
ISBN 978-0-00-719776-7

北京市版权局著作权合同登记号：01-2017-7645

责任编辑：王冬军　张丽丽　　　封面设计：李　一
责任校对：宋　夏　　　　　　　装帧设计：TOPTREE ctstoptree.com

出版发行：化学工业出版社（北京市东城区青年湖南街 13 号 邮政编码 100011）
印　　装：鸿博昊天科技有限公司
787mm×1092mm　1/16　印张 7 3/4　字数 256 千字
2018 年 5 月北京第 1 版第 4 次印刷

购书咨询：010-64518888（传真：010-64519686）
售后服务：010-64518899
网　　址：http: //www.cip.com.cn
凡购买本书，如有缺损质量问题，本社销售中心负责调换。

定　　价：49.00 元　　

写在前面的话

这本书献给全世界的所有孩子：献给他们所拥有的惊人的思维力以及无限的创造力。

特别要对在本书写作过程中提供帮助的“思维导图小作者”表示感谢：埃德蒙·特里维廉－约翰逊、亚历山大·基恩、亚历克斯·布兰迪斯、迈克尔·柯林斯，以及来自苏格兰（Berryhill School in Scotland）、美国（Willow Run School in Detroit）、新加坡（Singapore's Learning and Thinking Schools）、澳大利亚（Seabrook Primary School in Australia）的各所学校的孩子们。最后，要把感谢献给世界各地所有的思维导图小读者们！

目录

第四章　帮你牢记事物的诀窍

第五章　秀出你的记忆力

掌控记忆力，收获精彩人生

东尼·博赞致小读者信

当你有一天能够记住所有自己想记住的事情时，你会做什么？你是不是想——

★成为自己最崇拜的流行偶像或是世界一流的专家？

★记住本赛季每场足球赛的比分，让伙伴们对你钦佩不已？

★记住所有最棒的笑话，成为一个喜剧演员般十分有趣的人？

★了解与星球、行星相关的一切，成为受人敬仰的天文学家？

★成为著名演员，可以轻松背出剧本里的所有台词？

★记住历史上诸多的惊人事件，成为杰出的学者？

当你能够牢记很多事情时，就可以得到任何你想得到的东西。

这是一本可以助你实现上述愿望的书。我将教你如何利用一种神奇的记忆法来增强记忆力。你很快就会发现，当自己能牢记很多事情时，那些梦寐以求的东西就会纷至沓来：学习的效率飞速提高，有更多可支配的时间与朋友们一起玩；考场上游刃有余，每科都能轻松拿到 A；在自己非常感兴趣的领域博闻强识，甚至有同龄人来向你讨教如何才能更好地记忆。

这其中最棒的是什么呢？当然是运用你的记忆力，这其实是件很有意思的事。你的记忆力跟你一样，也希望能得到乐趣并好好享受一番。当你知道了要如何与它玩耍时，你将发现，每件事都变得非常有趣——即使现在的你一点都不觉得如此。

学无止境，而你的潜力是无穷的！拥抱你惊人的记忆力，将所有的美梦都变成现实吧！

所以，你还在等什么？赶快翻开这本书，准备好增强你的记忆力与专注力吧！ Let's go !

东尼·博赞

第一章

你拥有不可思议的记忆力

你是否知道自己拥有一种无限能力，它可以帮助你记住所有事情或者你想要记住的任何事情？

没错，任何事情！

想想看，你的人生将变得多么轻松并充满乐趣！伙伴们会觉得你超酷，因为你能记住球队每场比赛的比分；即使手机弄丢了，你也不会感到困扰，因为你记得通讯录中的所有电话号码；你应付考试也越来越得心应手，因为你记得所有学过的知识点——想一下，考出好成绩竟然变得如此容易！

在进行深入讨论之前，先想一想你会如何形容自己的记忆力。你觉得你是“记性好”还是“记性差”？你的记忆力是不是有时候很好，有时候却很差？举个例子，老师当着全班同学的面向你提问，是否有那么一瞬间，你的大脑一片空白，想不起任何东西？明明感觉自己是记得的，答案就悬在嗓子眼，可就是说不出来。最令人生气的是，你发现没有，过了一会儿，等你将头脑中这道记忆程序关闭，准备开始思考其他事情的时候，忽然又想起来答案了？

为什么会出现这种情况？如果你的记忆力总是让你失望，并不是因为你“很笨”、反应“迟钝”，或是其他任何你想到的可以用来形容自己的负面词语。这只是提醒你需要给记忆力一点帮助了，以便它能够更好地存储信息，并在需要它的时候能够回忆起那些信息。

想象你的大脑就是一座巨型图书馆吧！

神奇的大脑

大象永远不会忘记事情

大象拥有卓越的记忆力？千真万确！在经历了数年的分别之后，大多数的大象仍然能认出旧相识——它们的动物或人类朋友们。最近，有一群年轻的图利（位于南非博茨瓦纳的野生动物风景区）大象，在返回了南非的野生动物区后仍然能够认出它们的老朋友，继而很快就被象群所接纳，融入了新生活。

大脑中的信息一直存在，但如果这些信息零零散散地杂乱堆放，就很难被记起。你所需要做的，就是帮助你的大脑将这些信息有条理地储存起来，以便它们可以更容易地从脑海中被提取。这也是我想帮助你的地方。当你读完这本书的时候，你将可以轻松掌控自己的记忆力，记住任何想要记住的东西。

记忆女神之召唤

“记忆”这个词语的英文名是 memory，起源于一位希腊记忆女神的名字——摩涅莫辛涅（Mnemosyne）。她和天神宙斯共生了九个孩子，也就是九位缪斯。她们长大以后，分别成为掌管爱情诗、英雄史诗、颂歌、舞蹈、喜剧、悲剧、音乐、历史与天文的女神。

希腊人认为，只要结合宙斯的能力和摩涅莫辛涅的记忆力，就会产生知识和创意（对应九位缪斯所掌管的领域）。如果你擅长运用记忆技巧，就能增强记忆力，同时也会产生更多的创意，更快地学会新事物。

神奇的大脑

你知道的越多，你能积累的知识就越多

记忆力就像肌肉，锻炼的次数越多，就会变得越强大，而记忆事物本身也会变得越简单。随着记忆容量的增大，你能记住越来越多的事情。举个例子，大城市的出租车司机大脑中的海马体①比大多数人都要大，因为他们必须清晰地记得城市中绕来绕去的每一条路线。

①海马体，名称源于拉丁文“Hippocampus”，它形状似海马，是大脑中用来处理可视化思维的重要部分。

神奇的大脑

突破纪录的记忆力

目前为止，世界上记忆不同扑克牌数目最多的纪录，是 54 副经过洗牌后交错的 2808 张牌面！创造这个惊人纪录的是夺得 8 次世界脑力锦标赛冠军、来自英国的多米尼克·奥布莱恩（Dominic O'Brien）。他将 2000 多张扑克牌看过一遍之后，便能惊人地复述出它们的花色和数字。

奥林匹克思维

自古希腊时代以来，就有一些人因为展现出惊人的记忆力，而给周围人留下了极其深刻的印象。举例来说，他们可以依照不同的顺序，记住前后几百种事物——日期、数字、名字、脸孔，甚至准确无误地记住按不同顺序排列的几百张扑克牌！

难道他们拥有超能力？你或许会很惊讶地发现，他们其中的大部分人其实都是运用特别的“神奇记忆法”来帮助记忆的。

这些“神奇记忆法”动用了记忆力中的两支“明星队伍”，它们是：

1. 想象力
2. 联想力

如果想记住一些事情，你只需要先将其联想（串联）到某些你已经知道的事情，然后再运用想象力来记忆。想象力和联想力能确保你每次考试都得到高分。本章中我会一一告诉你运用想象力和联想力来提高考试分数的具体方法。

神奇的大脑

“抛接球”玩转左右脑

你会杂耍“抛接球”吗？“抛接球”不仅很有趣，而且还是一种能让左脑和右脑同时发挥功能的极佳方法。事实上，“抛接球”能增强你的记忆力，尤其是专注力（见第 36~37 页）。

左右脑模式提升记忆力

你知道人类大脑是由左、右两个区域构成的吗？这两个区域有着不同的功能以及不同的运作方式：当你在思考语言、数字或是清单时，你的左脑在发挥着作用；当你在观察颜色、学唱最喜爱的歌曲，或者为生日派对设想一个主题时，你的右脑开始发挥功效了。

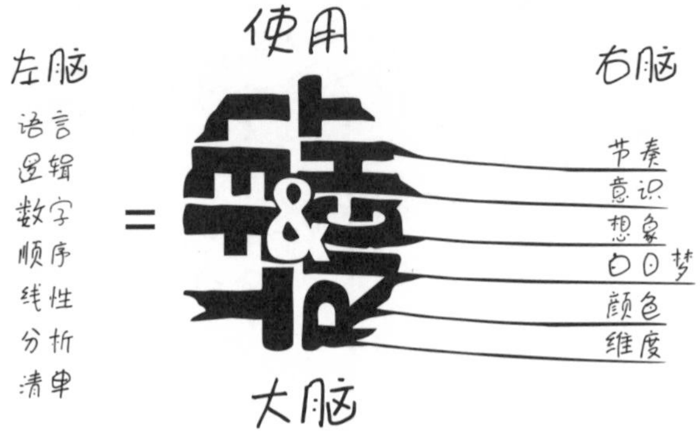

当你在学习或者记忆事物时，运用想象力之所以那么重要的原因，是你可以借此更好地使用右脑，而通常情况下你使用的是左脑。在学校里，你需要通过记忆来学习的事物有很多——日期、数字以及各类事件，这些都是左脑所擅长的。但如果你只使用一边的大脑，长此以往，这就好像你仅仅在用一条脚踝和手束缚在一起的腿拼命地往前走！

但如果你同时使用左右脑，这就像是一个团队在协同工作，不仅走起来更加轻松，而且还可以用最短的时间冲刺到终点，甚至超过终点线！这样一来，记住任何事情对你来说都是小菜一碟。

8
?
oui
si
ja
你好
7

想象力

充分发挥想象力，会让记忆变得更加有趣。你会发现，事情变得越有趣，就越容易记住。这里列举两组词汇：

1. 石头、空白、你的、白色、家庭作业、伴随
2. 派对、音乐、家长、假日、礼物、阳光

这两组词汇，哪一组比较好记呢？当然是能够引起你兴趣或听起来就十分有趣的那一组。对于那些你不喜欢的或是无法引发想象力的事物，你总是很容易忘记。而关键就在于如何运用想象力将自己想要记住的事物变得更加有趣，即便你觉得它们其实很无聊。现在，让我们看看在想象力这支队伍中，还有哪些明星队员呢？

★夸张。让我们面对这个事实——如果让你学习中世纪农作物的轮作种植，这看起来很不吸引人。不过，如果让想象力任意驰骋，你就可以让它变得很有意思。例如，你可以想象每年岁末，农作物从土壤里面跳出来，疯狂地跑到周围的农田里去！

★大笑。大笑、笑话、夸张是同一类别。当你把需要学习的知识想象得越滑稽、越令人吃惊时，你就越容易记住它们。所以，你可以想象麦子冲进邻近的田地时，竟然还冒着一股烟（哈哈，原来爆米花就是这么来的！），而且还大汗淋漓，气喘吁吁。

★感官。最大限度地利用你的五种感官，给想象力插上翱翔的翅膀。现在请你尽可能生动地想象一下农田里的情景："看见"长在田地里的金黄色麦穗，感受那种用手"触摸"它们时粗糙的感觉，"闻到"潮湿的泥土气味，"听见"麦子在另一片农田里互相摩擦发出的"沙沙"声，"品尝"谷物所特有的甜甜的味道。

什么是轮作种植

在中世纪，农民们每年都会改变农田里种植的作物，这样土壤中的养分才不会被耗尽。如果头年种的是小麦，下一年就会改种大麦，而第三年不种任何东西，让土地休耕。

★颜色。请想象这样一幅风景，并试着为它涂上最灵动的颜色：金黄色的麦田是如此的明亮，以至于你不得不把视线转向空旷田野中黑色的土壤，让你的眼睛歇上一歇，或者你眺望一片绿油油的麦田，看着麦子随微风摇曳。

★节奏。当你在学习时，如果能想象一些动作或者节奏，你的脑海中就会浮现出更加具体的图像。试着去想象所有的谷物们被连根拔起，它们急速跑到附近的农田里，而农夫们匆忙地在田埂间跑来跑去，像驱赶羊群那样让谷物们归队。

★积极思考。一般来说，你会更倾向于记住那些你喜欢的或是积极的事物，而不是那些不喜欢的或者消极的事物。所以，请不要再对自己说“我绝对不能忘记这件事”，而是要告诉自己“我一定会记住它”。当你开始不再为自己的记忆力担心时，你的机遇就来了！

神奇的大脑

一段关于大脑的简短历史

你是否知道：

★地球大约 ⟶ 有 50 亿年的历史？

★地球上开始出现第一个生命，大约 ⟶ 是在 40 亿年前？

★人类进化出“现代大脑”，大约 ⟶ 是在 10 万年前？

★人类终于知道大脑位于头部而不是心脏处，大约 ⟶ 是在 500 年前？

以及

★人类发掘了大脑 95% 的功能，大约 ⟶ 有 10 年的历史？

另外，科学家们还计算出，人类平均使用大脑的记忆功能还不到 1%。没错，1% 都不到。想想看，这对你来说意味着什么？想想看，你的大脑还有 99% 的空间被闲置，而你完全没用到它。这足以说明你真的可以记住每一件事情，而且是你想要记住的任何事情！

让你和你的记忆力，
一起开心地玩耍吧！

联想力

记忆力的第二支“明星队伍”是什么？当然是联想力。

联想就是将自己所知道的事物通通串联起来的方法。例如，当你回到母校拜访时，可能闻到某种特殊的气味，或者看到某些特定的事物，听到某些熟悉的声音，这些都能够让你想起当年，唤起你对母校栩栩如生的记忆。你可以准确无误地记起所有的事情。事实上，这些记忆一直储存在你的大脑里，而气味与声音的作用就像是“触发器”一样，启动了你的“记忆肌”开始运作。这样的联想既有趣又轻松，而且还会让你的想象力得到延伸。

你可以运用这种天生的大脑功能，来帮助自己学习和记忆新事物。你的联想力就像是一个摆满衣架的衣柜，如果你想学习新的事物，就必须先找出新事物与衣柜里面某样东西的关联，然后把它们挂在同一个衣架上。

比方说你参加一个派对，遇到了一个名叫亚历克斯的人，你希望能记住他的名字。刚好你弟弟也叫亚历克斯，而且他是个玩滑板的高手。那么，你就可以想象他们两个人一起玩滑板的场景。如果你能把在派对上认识的亚历克斯和你弟弟亚历克斯之间建立起强有力的联系，你就可以毫不费力地记住这位新的亚历克斯。此外，在联想力这支队伍中，还有哪些明星队员呢？

神奇的大脑
难以置信的惊人记忆力

你知道世界脑力锦标赛每年都会举办一次吗？在 2004 年的世界脑力锦标赛中，来自英国的本·普里德莫尔（Ben Pridmore）记住了一串由 3705 个“1”与“0”随机组合而成的数字（例如 1，0，0，1，1，0……），他打破了世界纪录，并赢得那一年脑力锦标赛的冠军！

★ 分类。找到你想记住事物的细分类别。举例来说，你要到商店里帮爸爸妈妈买东西，并且需要记住采购单上的所有物品。那么，你可以试着将它们分门别类，例如分成水果、蔬菜、肉类或者家用品。这样的过程就相当于把所有的信息分成了几个小部分。另外，你还可以找出其他的细分类别，例如根据大小尺寸（从大到小）、事情发生的时间（方便记忆的日期或者事件发生顺序）或者颜色分类等。

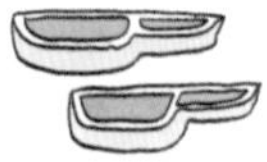

★ 数字。利用数字的大小顺序来帮助记忆。一些与数字密切相关的特殊记忆方法，我们会在第四章进行更深入的探讨。

★ 符号。利用符号或者图像为你的记忆力创造触发器，这是另一个聪明的方法。例如，每当你的脑海浮现出一个想法时，你可以在它的下面画上一个灯泡，或者当某些事情进展得很顺利时，你可以在它旁边画上一个笑脸。下一章你将会看到，思维导图就用到了很多的符号与图像。

现在，你已经知道，想象力和联想力，这两支记忆力的明星队伍可以帮助你获得成功。那么接下来，我们将要讨论记忆工具，以及如何提升你超凡的记忆力。

第二章

思维导图是最棒的记忆工具

思维导图是一种可供你选择的工具，能够帮助你将记忆力调整到最佳状态。思维导图之所以可以发挥极大的功效，是因为它充分利用了记忆力的两支“明星队伍”——想象力和联想力。

最棒的记忆工具

思维导图是协助大脑记录、计划，让你更轻松地记忆事物的一种奇妙方法。它使用颜色、图像让你的记忆力尽情驰骋，你可以借由这些颜色与图像之间的关联、曲线或者“分支”，使用文字或图像把思维导图描绘出来，帮助记忆力产生强有力的联想。

利用思维导图记忆任何事情，不论是多么复杂的事情，都会像刮一阵微风一样轻松。它就是你最棒的记忆工具！

思维导图能够帮助你

★ 记住是谁借了你的 CD；
★ 记得需要携带的所有度假物品；
★ 分神时仍然可以集中注意力；
★ 更好地做课堂笔记；
★ 记住家人及朋友的生日；
★ 从不同的渠道（网络、图书馆、博物馆等）做研究并获得信息；
★ 复习功课以备战考试；
★ 记得做过的梦。

如何绘制思维导图

绘制思维导图其实很容易。

让我们以你的那个相当酷的假期为例。即使那时你度过了一段非常美好的时光，可一旦回到学校，假期时光似乎就变得离你很遥远了。甚至当别人在你刚回来时，问你假期做了些什么，你竟然想不起来了。

1. 拿出一张空白的纸（不要有线条，因为它会妨碍你思绪的流动性），把纸张横过来放。

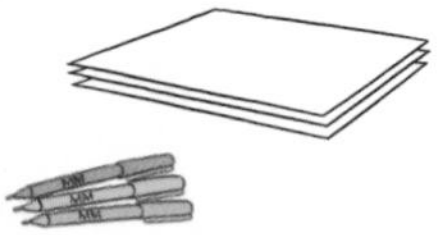

2. 拿出几支彩笔，选出你最喜欢的几种颜色。

3. 在白纸中央画出你在度假时做了什么或者到了哪里等等有关的图像，然后在图像的上方、下方或者里面写上“我的假期”。把你的思绪放在中心图像上，保持注意力集中，让思绪自由地延伸。

4. 选择不同颜色的彩笔，围绕中心图像分别画出由粗到细的大纲主干。然后写下你对假期的第一个最深刻的印象，只用简单的关键词来表达即可，接下来，再写出几个不同的印象，把全部内容分支进行填充。

以麦克的思维导图为示例，他刚从国外度假回来，我们能看出，围绕他假期的几个大纲主干分别是活动、人们、酒店、远足、海滩。如法炮制，你也可以绘制自己假期的思维导图，围绕自己的中心图像，用不同的颜色画出几个大纲主干。

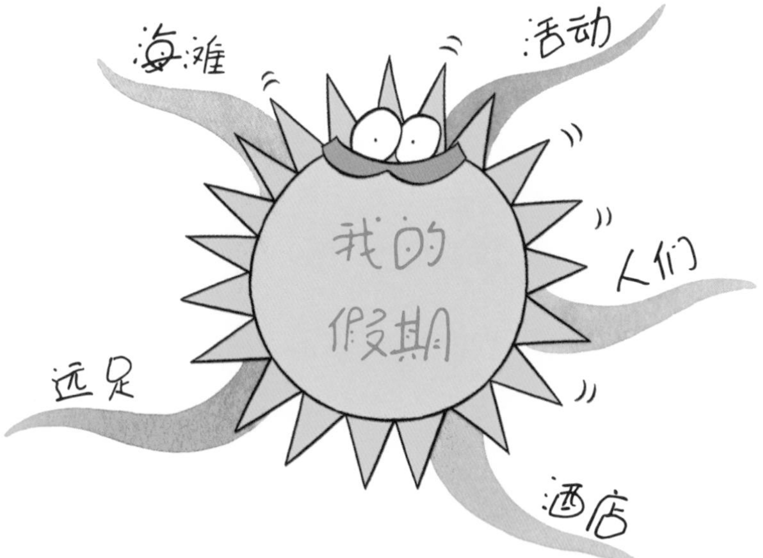

5. 现在，请你开动脑筋好好想一下，你在自己的导图中应该画出哪些大纲主干。如果其中一个大纲主干是海滩，那么你在海滩上做了什么呢？游泳？日光浴？盖沙堡？你还可以在大纲主干上再画出几个细小的分支，然后用比较小的字把想到的事情写上去。你可以在你认为非常重要的每个细小的分支旁边都画上插图或符号（图像语言有助于你发挥想象力）。简单的素描也是不错的选择——没错，如果你会的话。一定要让这些关键词与图像同你的分支产生关联，只要它们在纸上产生了关联，就会在你的大脑里也产生关联，这些分支通过联想力来帮助记忆。

6. 如果你的大脑中浮现出更多的相关想法，请为这些次级的想法增加更多的分支。现在，你已经对假期有一个完整的记录了。这就像写日记一样，而且比写日记还要棒！那么，请你翻到第 22 ～ 23 页，看看麦克在他的假期里都做了些什么吧。

神奇的大脑

做梦吧

你知道吗？夜间的美梦和白日梦都可以帮助你发挥想象力，并有助于提高记忆力。

脑力测试

1. 帮助记忆力提升的两支“明星队伍”分别是?

2. 在这两支队伍中，都有哪些队员?

3. 哪个字母在一周内会出现 2 次，一年内会出现 1 次，但是一天内从来不会出现?

4. 一年只上一天班，而且永远不会担心被炒鱿鱼的人是谁?

答案：

1. 想象力和联想力。

2. 夸张、大笑、感官、颜色、节奏、积极思考是想象力的组成元素。联想力的组成元素是分类、数字、符号。

3. 字母 e（week 中有 2 个 e，year 中有 1 个 e，day 中没有 e）。

4. 圣诞老人。

看书
日光浴
帆船运动
浮潜
烧烤
海滩
游泳
堆沙城堡
博物馆
城堡
远足
咖啡馆
纪念碑
走路
购物
脚踏船
遮阳伞
躺椅
跳舞
我
假

水肺
岩石
爬山
潜水
风筝
放飞
活动
足球
室内足球
妈妈
爸爸
家人
朱迪
人们
吉姆
胡安
朋友
导游
微笑
凯利
戴夫
出租车
洛克伍德
迪多
酒店
萨姆
皮纳斯酒店
游泳池
王朝酒店
沙滩排球
健身房

“我的假期”思维导图

让你的思想起飞

如果现在学校让你提交一份关于“火药的阴谋”的历史方案，你一定会通过图书馆、网络和当地的博物馆去收集资料，并且在找资料的过程中做许多笔记。然后，你必须有条理地把资料整合起来，并且记住这些资料的内容，以便你在课堂上侃侃而谈。那么现在，让我们看看你的笔记还存在些什么问题。

你该如何整合这么多的资料呢？虽然有很多种不同的整理资料的方法，但你很难确定哪种最好，这时候，你可以尝试把你认为可以归类的资料放在思维导图的大纲主干中。例如，你的笔记中有很多关于宗教的部分，这可以作为思维导图中的大纲主干之一。此外，在资料中也有关于阴谋本身的内容以及涉及到的一些相关的故事，那么，阴谋也可以构成其中的一个大纲主干。

思维导图鼓励你运用联想力找出信息之间的相关性，帮助你恰当地汇总信息，这也正是它之所以能提高记忆力的原因。当你绘制完一幅思维导图后，你会发现原来可以把所有的信息都集中在一张纸上。够酷吧！请参照第28～29页的思维导图示例，看看你能否绘制出属于自己的思维导图。

如果你想在讨论课上记住所有的分享信息，可以在大脑中想象一幅思维导图，想象它的每一个大纲主干和内容分支，并且记住它们的颜色与位置。这样，你就可以把所有线条的颜色、位置和所包含的信息联系在一起了。用过几次这种方法后，你就可以不费吹灰之力地记住所有信息。

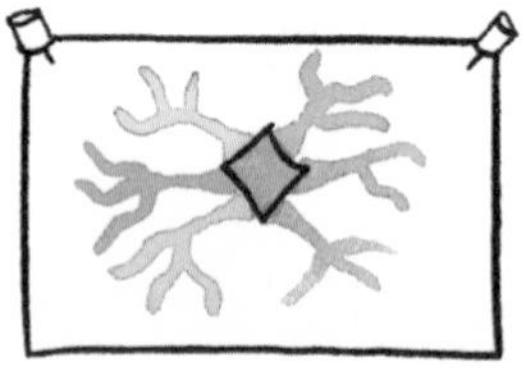

1

1605年的火药阴谋事件，差点炸毁整个英国议会大厦。

2

在英国女王伊丽莎白一世去世后，苏格兰国王詹姆士六世作为与她血缘关系最近的家族成员，继承了王位，成为英国国王詹姆士一世，同时也是英国国教领袖。

3

当时英国的基督教主要有三个派系——视教皇为领袖的罗马天主教；视英国国王为领袖的英国国教；以及追寻纯净，试图摒弃主教、蜡烛、长袍和仪式的清教。

4

当时的天主教徒认为，天主教将会东山再起，他们能选出自己的领袖并统治全国。

5

天主教会以及由罗伯特·盖茨比所带领的一小部分人，包括盖伊·福克斯等人非常讨厌詹姆士一世，决定谋杀他和所有议会成员。

6

天主教徒们租下了一间与英国议会大厦相邻的房子，同时挖出一条通往议会大厦地下室的地道，并在那里放置了几十桶炸药，准备在国王与上议院、下议院议员出现时炸死所有人。

7

由于有背叛者偷偷向上议院议员蒙特伊格发出警告，消息不胫而走，当议员们带人搜查地下室时，他们当场逮捕了盖伊·福克斯。

8

福克斯被带到伦敦塔，使用严刑逼供，但他始终没有供出其他参与者。最后，他和其他被捕的天主教徒共八人被判处死刑。

9

此后，在每年的11月5日，英国人都会燃放焰火，纪念议会大厦的幸存。燃烧的火焰呈现出当年那场阴谋中炸药的威力。由于盖伊·福克斯是被烧死的，所以焰火的顶端会放置一个假人，叫作"傻瓜"福克斯。

神奇的大脑

记住哪一天

你是不是总记不住哪天要做什么事情？没关系，在思维导图上画出想要记住的具体日期（几月几号或星期几），你就能轻而易举地记住在正确的时间、地点做正确的事情了。

恭喜你！现在你已经掌握了最棒的记忆工具——思维导图。在你继续阅读下一章之前，不妨鼓掌并休息一下——这是你对自己的奖励！

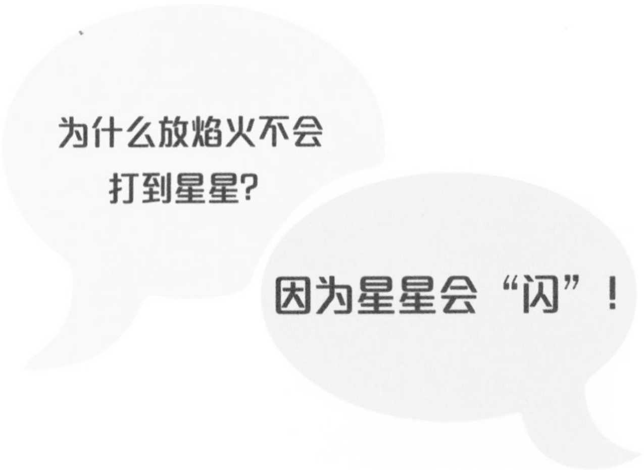

脑力测试

1. 当你走进一个黑漆漆的房间时，你的手上只有一根火柴，房间里面有一盏油灯，一个暖炉和一个炉灶。你会先点燃什么？

2. 两对父子去买帽子，为什么只买了三顶？

3. 什么东西洗好了以后放在桌上却不会被吃掉？

4. 你一整天都在问别人同一个问题，每次得到的正确答案都不一样，这个问题是什么呢？

答案：
1. 火柴。
2. 因为他们是爷爷、爸爸和儿子。
3. 扑克牌。
4. 时间。

“火药的阴谋”思维导图

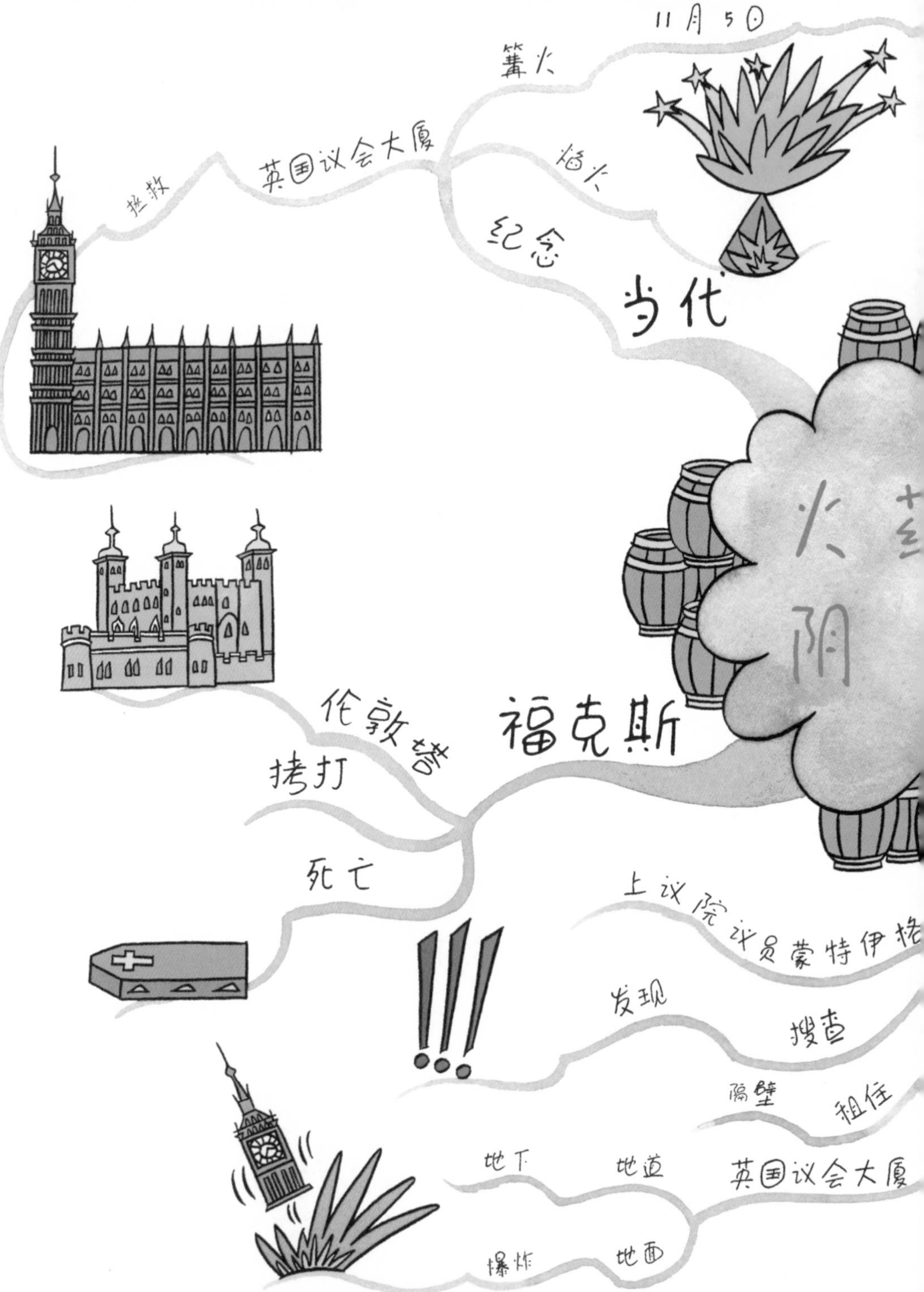
11月5日
篝火
英国议会大厦
挽救
焰火
纪念
当代
火
阴
伦敦塔
福克斯
拷打
死亡
上议院议员蒙特伊格
发现
搜查
隔壁
租住
地下
地道
英国议会大厦
爆炸
地面

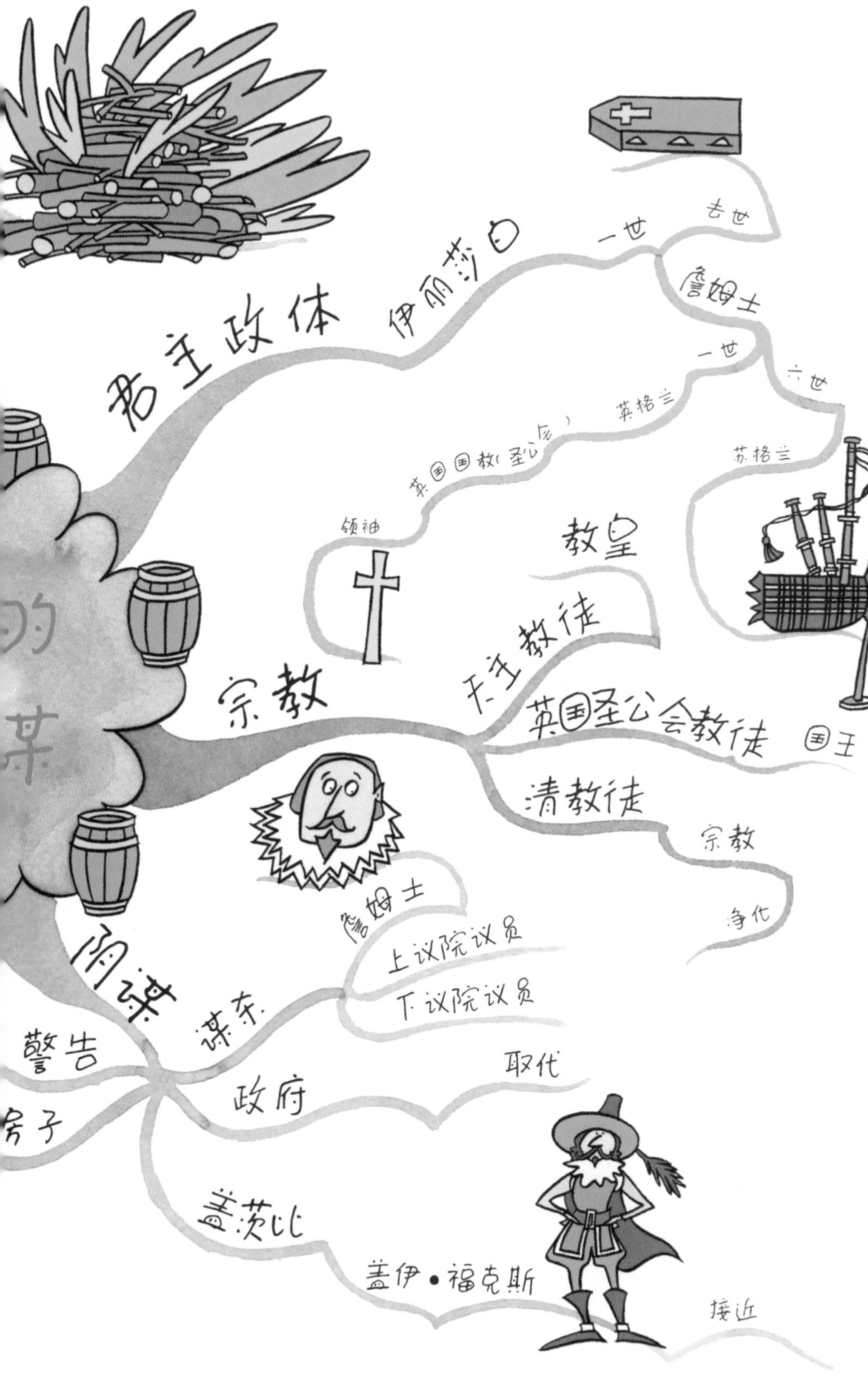
君主政体
伊丽莎白
一世
去世
詹姆士
一世
六世
英格兰
英国国教（圣公会）
苏格兰
领袖
宗教
教皇
天主教徒
英国圣公会教徒
国王
清教徒
宗教
净化
詹姆士
上议院议员
下议院议员
阴谋
谋杀
警告
政府
取代
盖茨比
盖伊·福克斯
接近

第三章

复习与休息，让你记得更好

休息并不仅仅是简单的放松。信不信由你，在休息的状态下，你其实能学得更好！

休息的状态下往往能学习得更好。因为当你在做一些看似与学习无关的事的同时，大脑其实在忙碌地工作！

你也许觉得不可思议，但这个事实可以帮助你解决很多问题。因为即便是休息时，大脑仍然在帮助你归档信息，以便你在需要它们的时候可以及时找到。很酷吧？一旦大脑储存了一批信息，接下来就会准备储存下一批信息。记住，记忆力总是渴望记住更多的东西，所以，大脑也需要一些时间，来给自己留出空间，以便更妥善地保存好这些信息。

神奇的大脑

休息的好处

你是否注意到，有很多很棒的主意都是在不经意间冒出来的？

你是如何想到举办生日派对时那些超酷超炫的点子的？在你的浴缸里！

你是怎么想出数学题答案的？在你从学校回家的路上！

全世界所有的天才也同你一样，常常在不经意间冒出灵感！

实际上，当大脑充分休息时，正是它发挥出最佳功能的时刻。所以，当你陷入对某个问题的困惑与不解中时，不如站起来，出去走一走，去做一些别的事情吧。

休息有利于更好地记忆

首先需要明确，这里我们提到的休息是哪一种？当你在家的时候，你可以充分掌握和规划自己的时间，无论是写家庭作业，还是复习迎考，或者纯粹为了兴趣而学习。当你感觉大脑疲倦时，可以短暂地休息 5 ～ 10 分钟。当然，最好能休息 45 分钟左右。你可以走出去呼吸一些新鲜空气，或者玩玩球（例如第 36 ～ 37 页的“抛接球”游戏），或者走到另一个房间，做些与现在手头上的事情无关的其他事情。当你回来的时候，你将会神清气爽，迫不及待地继续开始学习。

看一看下图中“遗忘之河”上的两条绳子。最下面的那条，代表你在24 小时内一直学习而不休息的状态下的记忆程度。看绳子深深陷入河谷的中间部分，想象你需要费多大力气才能拉住它！而其中大部分的记忆都将掉落到遗忘之河中，被鱼儿吃掉。至于上面的那条绳子，两个拉绳子的人则轻松得多。他们在河床里建起许多根柱子，让绳子可以一直维持在横跨河流上方的状态。而每根柱子都代表了一小段休息时间。他们的绳子一直在遗忘之河的上方，他们的记忆不会掉落到河中，因此，他们可以记住许多事情。

如何练习专注力

你是不是想练习专注力，却不知道从何入手？其实很简单，成为一个玩杂耍“抛接球”高手！你只需要三个小的、软的、同样大小与重量的球或者豆子，以及你的专注力和决心。

步骤 1：一个球

请你用一只手握住一个球，将双手放在与腰部水平的正前方位置，然后把手上的球，以抛物线的弧度向上抛，直至球落到另外一只手中。

重复这个动作，让手上的球来回保持在抛掷状态，直到你可以不经思考地完成这个动作。

小技巧：从你的手肘处正前方位置开始抛球，而不是从腰部。请你面朝墙壁持续练习下去，直到你完全掌握向上抛球的诀窍。

步骤 2：两个球

现在，左右手各拿一个球。请把 1 号球（右手的）以抛物线的弧度向上抛至左手。当球到达最高点时（球最高点与眼睛齐平），请开始把 2 号球（左手的）向上抛至你的右手。然后依次用左手接住 1 号球，用右手接住 2 号球，停住。

请你开始重复做一次这个动作，不过这次不是从你的右手，而是从你的左手开始做起，直到你可以不慌不忙地把球顺畅地在两手之间抛来抛去。

步骤 3：三个球

现在用你最灵活的手（右手，如果你是左撇子就用左手）拿住 1 号和 3 号球，另外一只手拿 2 号球。然后开始，将 1 号球（以右手为例，放在右手前端）以抛物线的弧度，抛向你的左手。

当 1 号球达到最高点时，开始将 2 号球以抛物线的弧度抛向你的右手

（与步骤 2 一致）。

当 2 号球达到最高点时，请你把右手的 3 号球以同样的方式抛向你的左手，并同时用右手接住 2 号球。

小技巧：在抛 3 号球之前，让它在手中转动一下，这样会简单很多。

当 3 号球到达最高点时，将 1 号球抛至右手。然后再用左手接住 3 号球。像这样再练一次，并且持续练习下去。

杂耍“抛接球”的重要提示：

★ 永远将球以抛物线的弧度抛掷；
★ 将两只手保持在腰部的高度；
★ 使用不同颜色的球，这样更利于分辨；
★ 把球向上抛至约与眼睛齐平的高度；
★ 千万别想一次就成功，慢慢来，多练习；
★ 不断地练习，练习，再练习。

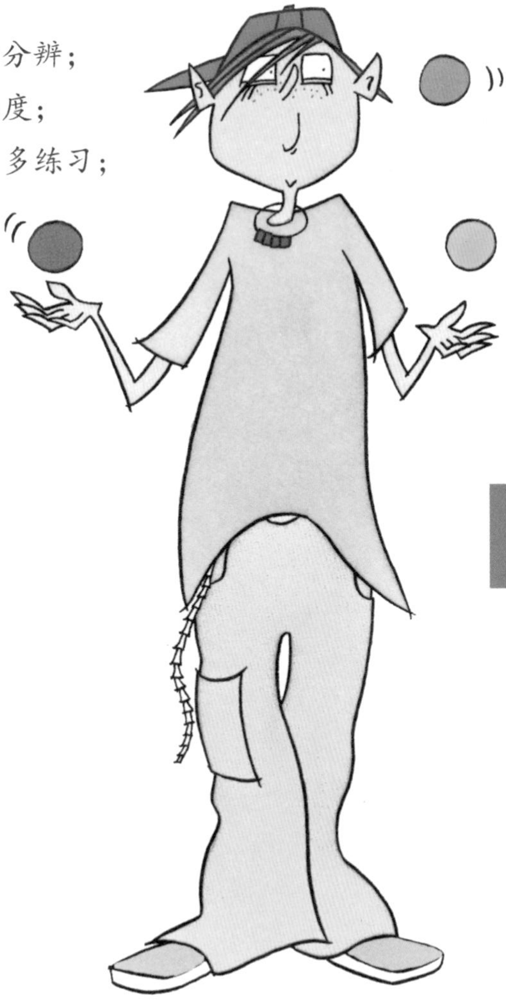

留意心智反应

你是否发现，一篇课文的开头要比中间部分更加容易记忆。在听课的过程中，除非你能运用联想力把课堂学习的东西串联在一起，或是老师教的内容确实很特别，否则你真的很容易走神。一直到快要下课时，你的大脑才会又活跃起来，而且只有这时你才会比较轻松地记住知识点。

我们可以用下一页的水位图来说明这个观点。水位一开始比较高，然后落下来一点，接着又高起来。学习的最高点，则是图上的三个明显的大波浪（也就是可以把事物串起来的地方），以及那个冲浪男孩（他很特别！）。就像前文“遗忘之河”上方的那条绳子，如果你可以给自己留出一些休息时间，让心智维持一个平稳的状态，这样反而更利于学习。要知道，在“心智空间”最不容易集中精神的时候，就算有再多信息，你也记不住一丁点儿。

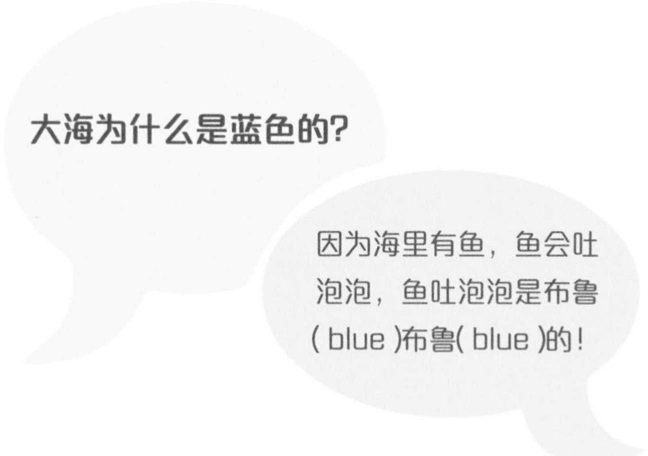

大海为什么是蓝色的?
因为海里有鱼，鱼会吐泡泡，鱼吐泡泡是布鲁（blue）布鲁（blue）的！

"心智空间"水位图

神奇的大脑

你知道在你的大脑里面有 1 万亿个脑细胞吗？脑细胞非常小，100 个脑细胞大概只有针尖那么一丁点儿大。如果你把大脑中所有的脑细胞排成一排，它的长度可以从地球延伸至月球再绕回地球。你知道吗？月球距离地球大约有 384400 千米！

注意力之驹

冷静也是集中注意力的好方法。你必须集中注意力，才可以正确地学习知识。想象一下，你的注意力就像是一匹强健的骏马——既高大又活泼，蓄势待发的马。而你已经准备好要驾驭它！就像这样，当它愿意被你驾驭，而你也希望这么做时，你可以不费吹灰之力骑上它。但有时候，它却并不配合，不想按照任何人说的话去做。就好比，当你在做白日梦的时候，你宁愿想象自己是一个电影明星，也不会去想应该如何解决几何习题。

神奇的大脑

你是否知道，大脑的不同区域分别掌管着不同的任务？在你的大脑中，掌管记忆的区域是最大的部分，而且它就像是一个巨大的浴帽，覆盖了大脑的其他区域。你的大脑是一个层叠的、充满褶皱的组织，它是由两个不同的半球——左半球与右半球构成的。所以，当人们说大脑有两边，意思是说，大脑可以分为左脑和右脑。

大象的左耳朵像什么？

它的右耳朵！

你的注意力像一匹脱缰的野马一样四处狂奔，在各种事物之间跳来跳去。虽然让注意力之驹狂奔是一件很有趣的事，但你还是必须知道，应该如何解决讨厌的几何习题。如果说你的注意力之驹是一匹顶级的赛马，那么你所要做的就是学会如何成功地驾驭它，然后在最关键的时刻将它用在最重要的事情上，以使自己遥遥领先于其他人。怎样才能做到这一点呢？你必须放飞想象力。

拯救想象力

有时候，你发现在上课时很难集中注意力，这是因为当需要你发挥想象力的时候，你却做不到。请试着按照下面的建议来拯救你的想象力。

★绘制一幅思维导图，以你正在学习的某篇课文为主题。这能够帮助你发挥自己的想象力，并且集中注意力，让你不再分心。此外，思维导图还能帮助你轻松记住课文内容。如果你愿意，请带上一幅空白的思维导图到学校，以便可以在听课的过程中将知识点标注到上面。

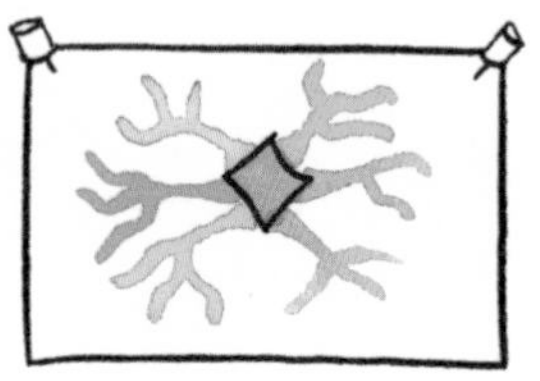

★试着运用本书第四章中讲到的各种记忆工具。举例来说，如果你需要记住很多的日期，你可以使用“数字－形状法”或者“数字－韵律法”来激发自己的想象力；如果你正在读一段很枯燥的文字，你可以采用“记忆电影”来增加这段文字的趣味性。

★找机会提问或者回答问题。如果你能够完全融入到课文的意境中去，你的想象力就会助你一臂之力，让你更加容易地学习以及理解课文。

★如果你对某个科目一点都不感兴趣，你可以运用想象力，把这个科目与能够吸引你注意力的其他事情串联在一起。举例来说，你是不是对语文完全没兴趣？但你不是很喜欢跟朋友聊天吗？不信的话，请检查一下你的社交软件的聊天记录吧！是的！语文和聊天很接近，而且相关联！天才剧作家莎士比亚都是在与人聊天，或者聆听别人谈话的过程中找到灵感的，所以才能写出那些精彩的故事和剧本。所以你看，如果你想要通过与朋友畅谈来吸引别人的注意力，你就必须得对语文感兴趣！

什么英文字母是人们喜欢听的而且听的人最多?
CD！

救命啊！遇到考试大脑一片空白

通常当你感觉压力很大时，大脑很容易一片空白。例如，老师当着全班同学的面向你提问，你却什么都想不起来了。这真是糟糕透了。如果这种情况发生在考场，那绝对是一场噩梦。

遇到这种情况时，首先要放轻松。在非常紧张的时刻，用你的想象力让自己不那么害怕——只需放松几秒钟，否则，大脑空白的感觉会一直跟随着你。举例来说，当你打开考卷，必须回答一个关于重力的问题时，如果你紧盯着试题，反而什么都想不起来。

这里教你一些摆脱“大脑一片空白”，找到解题路径的办法：

★ 闭上眼睛，将手放至腹部，慢慢、深深地吸气——吐气——吸气，感觉到腹部一缩一鼓。

★ 几秒种后，思绪回到考卷上。一心想着关键词——重力。当然，你肯定知道重力就是让你的双脚保持在地面上的力。

★ 在开了个好头之后，请你快速绘制一幅思维导图草稿，让想象力朝着正确方向发挥。你知道不同的行星有不同的重力，比如月球，想必你看过许多航天员在月球表面跳来跳去的海报。请你把这个信息也放在导图中。

★ 继续使用思维导图自问自答。你会发现所有信息都重新浮现在脑海中，而且如果你在修改导图的时候加入了有关重力的部分，你会发现你记住了导图中的每个分支。

建议：如果你使用该方法 1 ～ 2 分钟后，还是没效果，请你先开始回答其他问题。这时候，你的记忆仍然会努力寻找第一道问题的答案。等你回过头再解答它时，答案应该已经从脑海中冒出来了。

每件事情想 5 遍

有时候，你会发现，明明很了解的某件事情，却忽然记不起来了，就好像从来没发生过一样。是不是很沮丧？不要急，你之所以会忘记这些事，是因为以前并没有对它们进行重复记忆的工作。

当你第一次接触某件事情时，它只会在你的大脑中留下短暂的印象。也就是说，你只能记住这件事情几分钟、几天，如果使用记忆工具，或许可以延长至几周。那么如果想永远地记住这件事情，该怎么做呢？你需要把短暂记忆转化为长期记忆，就像是定期地从头至尾再复习一遍所学的东西。

如果你使用本书中介绍的记忆工具持续地去重复记忆，你只需从头至尾反复想 5 遍，就可以永远记住它了。想想看，当临近考试的时候，这将为你省下来多少精力和时间，免除多少担心？那么，该如何进行重复记忆呢？

重复想 5 遍 = 长期记忆

第 1 遍：你第一次了解它的时候；
第 2 遍：你第一次了解它后的第 2 天；
第 3 遍：你第一次了解它的 1 周后；
第 4 遍：你第一次了解它的 1 个月后；
第 5 遍：你第一次了解它的 3~6 个月后。

当重复记忆 5 遍以后，你会发现你的创造力已经在“接手”这件事情了。你的想象力将在你学过并且记住的东西上大有一番作为，你发现自己知道的事情越来越多。这是因为，你已经在记忆库中建立了越来越多的关联。白日梦在这个时候特别管用，它让你的信息随着某个意念或者思绪尽情驰骋，这些意念和思绪会在脑海中变得越来越生动。

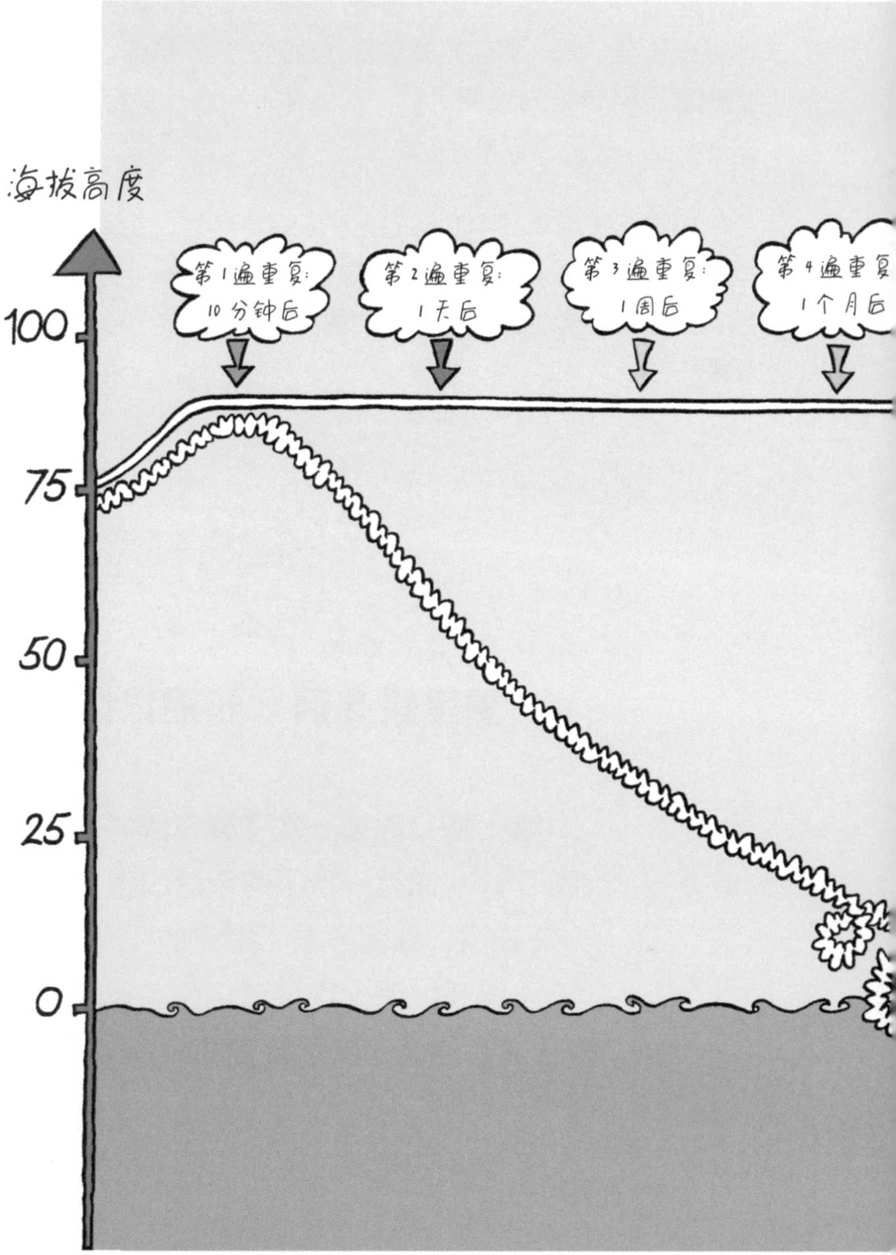

请仔细观察下图中的飞机。它显示了，当你从头至尾反复想一件事 5 遍后，会产生什么样的效果。那架坠落的红色飞机显示，如果缺少重复记忆的过程，你会在一开始就遗忘信息，并混淆大脑中所有的信息。因此，记忆的高度会一直下降，直至坠落。但是白色的飞机则一直保持在一定高度，而且可以往上飞，这代表你已经完全记住了这件事，还把它与你记住的其他事情联系在一起。你会发现，你能记住的事情越来越多。

坚持练习重复记忆

当你在进行重复记忆，或再次尝试重复记忆时，你需要花一点时间和功夫来整理信息，才能让这种记忆方法的功效发挥到极致。最好的办法就是买一本很大的彩色日历，习惯性地在上面写下你每天学到了什么。

请你花 20 分钟回想一下，这一天你在学校学到了什么，然后回头看一下日历中这个星期，这个月或者 6 个月以前你又学到了些什么。有哪些是需要你重复记忆的。把所有你不了解的事情都记下来，然后向同学、父母、老师请教。如果你坚持这么做的话，就永远不必担心考试前要临时抱佛脚了，因为你记得老师说过的每件事情。

脑力测试

1. 哪种光完全没有亮度?

2. 用的次数越多，它离我们越远，这是什么东西?

3. 三个人钓鱼，不小心船翻了。三个人掉进水里。但只有两个人头发湿了，为什么第三个人的头发没有湿?

4. “请你从我的头上拔掉一根头发，然后挠我的头。一开始我的头发是红的，后来会变成黑色，请你猜猜我是谁?”

答案:

1. 时光。
2. 脚印。
3. 因为第三个人是秃头。
4. 火柴。

第四章

帮你牢记事物的诀窍

现在，是教授你一些很棒的记忆工具的时候了。就像思维导图一样，这些工具也有两支“明星队伍”——想象力和联想力。

你可以单独使用它们，也可以结合思维导图使用。这些工具能让你的记忆过程变得更加有趣！所以，让思维更奔放、更大胆一点，让你在记忆的过程中笑声洋溢，让你整个人都变得与众不同吧！

对你而言，越是频繁地与记忆力玩耍，记忆事情就会变得越容易。

电影记忆法

“电影记忆法”是最容易上手的记忆工具之一。你所要做的，就是记录想象中的属于自己的电影剧情，然后尽可能地渲染它的五彩斑斓、它非常刺激的情节，以及夸张的人物角色。如果你充分使用了想象力，你就能轻而易举地记住电影中所有的人物和情节。想象自己现在是一部耗资上亿的大片的导演，就像《哈利·波特》《星球大战》《怪物史莱克》一样，你也可以为你的电影取一个吸引人的片名。同时，你必须重复播放它好几遍，以确保其中包含了你所需要的信息并且你已将它“保存”于大脑中某个恰当的位置。

还记得上一章讨论的重复记忆吗？当你需要回忆这些信息的时候，只需先找到脑海中的“大荧幕”，然后按下“播放键”，就行了。

电影记忆法帮助你随时记住

★ 你们足球队在所有获胜的比赛中的得分；

★ 与别人的冲突中所发生的事情以及挑起者是谁；

★ 跟随你最喜欢的节奏起舞的舞步；

★ 做你最喜爱的巧克力蛋糕所需的步骤；

★ 在某次科学实验中需要做的事情；

★ 自己绘制的思维导图（大致地重复想象一下思维导图中的大纲主干与内容分支，并在大脑中将信息演练一番）。

神奇的大脑
究竟是怎样的存在

你的大脑可以装下整个宇宙！这怎么可能？然而科学家已经证实，大脑能够存储的信息数量，比目前整个宇宙已知原子的数量还要多。

鱼为什么生活在水里？

因为陆地上有猫！

脑力测试

1. 树上有 100 只鸟，用什么方法才能把它们全部抓住?

2. 8 个人吃 8 份快餐需 10 分钟，16 个人吃 16 份快餐需几分钟?

3. 从前有一个很聪明的小偷，因为被指控叛国而被判处死刑。但是国王为了表现宽宏大量，让小偷自己选择死法。小偷会如何选择呢?

4. 什么东西没有脚却能带你游遍全世界?

答案：

1. 用照相机。
2. 还是 10 分钟。
3. 小偷选择随年龄增长自然死去。
4. 船。

灯光、摄影机都准备好了？开始拍摄！

请你回忆一下宇宙中的八大行星。你能够按照正确的排列顺序，指出这八颗行星吗？

你知道哪颗行星最大，哪颗行星最小吗？如果总记不住的话，使用电影记忆法，便可以解决这个问题，并且永远记住它们的排列顺序。

以下是太阳系中的八颗行星[1]，按照接近太阳的顺序依次排列：

1. 水星
2. 金星
3. 地球
4. 火星
5. 木星
6. 土星
7. 天王星
8. 海王星

如果你只是想死记硬背记住八大行星的排列，一定会累得满头大汗。你应该运用电影记忆法，启动你的想象力。

蝴蝶、蚂蚁、蜘蛛、蜈蚣在一起工作，最后，谁没有领到报酬？

蜈蚣！
（无功不受禄）

---

① 2006 年在捷克布拉格举行的第 26 届国际天文学联合会通过决议，冥王星不再被列为太阳系中的第九颗行星，它现被降级成“矮行星”。

咔，开始拍摄！

首先想象在你面前的是太阳，它是一个红彤彤、散发着灼热光芒的美丽球体。看一看、闻一闻并感受它的热量，观察它的鲜艳色彩，感觉到它变得越来越热。在太阳系中，前四颗行星体积小，后四颗行星体积大。

再想象一下，在太阳旁边的是一个小小的、充满了水银的温度计，它就是水星（Mercury，亦有“水银”的意思）。随着太阳变得越来越热，你看到温度计中的水银柱上升，直到最后，一声巨响，它爆炸了，留下一些小水银珠（当然，水星本来就是一个小行星）挂在空中。站在水星旁边的是一位美丽动人的小女神（第二个小行星）。用想象力给她配上色彩、香味、风格、着装，然后观察她。我们该叫它什么？金星维纳斯（Venes）。以古罗马的爱之神命名。

维纳斯拾起一个小水银球，运用神力扔出去，恰好丢在你所住地方的前面不远处。你住的地方在哪里呢？地球（Earth，亦有“土块”的意思）。为了让整个画面更加“真实”，想象一下水银球形成了一个小火山口，一些土块从中喷射而出，掉入你隔壁邻居的花园里。

在这个想象的故事中，你的邻居是一个身材矮小（最后一个小行星）、面红耳赤（它是一个红色行星）、怒气冲冲且好战的人物，他向你冲过来，手里还拿着一块巧克力棒。他就是火星马尔斯（Mars），古代神话中的战神。

火星马尔斯要走出来找麻烦，正好在大街上有一个巨人，他是诸神之王，100 多米高，也是至今为止最大的行星，前额上翘起的一绺头发像“J”。这就是木星朱庇特（Jupiter），他命令火星马尔斯停止发火并回到屋子里去。

你抬头看着朱庇特巨大的胸廓，看到他胸前的 T 恤上印着巨大的火焰字母 SUN。每个字母代表太阳系最后三个巨大行星的首字母：S 代表 SATURN（农神萨杜恩），土星；U 代表 URANUS（天空之神乌拉诺斯），天王星；N 代表 NEPTUNE（海神尼普顿），海王星。

好了，Cut！
电影拍完了！

现在，倒回去重放一遍电影。用你所有的感官重新再看一次，审视一次。你通过“拍电影”记录下的故事，能帮助你将八大行星的名称和排列顺序都记在脑中。

你是否已经都记下来了？都记住了？太棒了。如果还没有完全记住，那就在心里再放几遍电影，加强对影像的印象。

让我们回到电影里，把那些你不是很确定的部分记录下来，然后发挥你的想象力，加强那些影像在你脑海中的印象。运用你所有的感官，你会发现，神奇得就像变魔术一样，自己一下子都记住了！举例来说，如果你不确定金星的位置，就再次想象一位美丽的女神，她有着一头随风飘逸的金发。想象一下她穿的衣服——她可能穿着一件飘逸的白色长裙，长裙上还沾着温度计爆炸时留下的水银。

考试时我的大脑一片空白，怎么办

考试时，如果一下子忘记了要如何答题，怎么办？要镇定。让思绪慢慢回到当时正在学习的状态，那时你是坐在学校书桌前，还是在卧室中温习功课？那时你正在看哪一本书？看到了第几页？……你的思绪很喜欢通过位置来记忆，所以按照上面的方法来做，很可能唤起你的记忆，并且加深记忆（更多在紧张状态下唤醒记忆的小建议请看第 44 页）。

迷你记忆工具

这里我们使用“首字母缩略词”进行记忆。这是一种很简便的记忆方法。想想看，你只需要用想记住的词的第一个字母拼成其他词就可以了。简单吧？

举例来说，想记住北美五大湖：休伦（Huron）、安大略（Ontario）、密歇根（Michigan）、伊利（Erie）和苏必利尔（Superior）。你可以把几个湖的名称的首字母拼成 homes。如果你把它们和 homes 联系起来，只要想象一部迷你记忆电影的画面是几栋漂浮在湖面上的房子。记住那几栋漂浮在湖面上的房子，以及每一个湖泊名称的首字母和 homes 的字母顺序对应，你就可以轻松回忆起五大湖泊了！

六位女士，一位先生

现在，你可以尝试自己制作一部电影，用来记住亨利八世的六任妻子的顺序与名字，以及她们各自的命运：

阿拉贡的凯瑟琳——离婚
安妮·博林——处死
珍·西摩——去世
克里维斯的安妮——离婚
凯瑟琳·霍华德——处死
凯瑟琳·帕尔——存活

你可以使用任何你喜欢的方法制作电影，在开始之前，请先阅读下面的注意事项。请记住，在你的“记忆电影”里面没有所谓的“正确”的脚本——只要能捕捉想象力的灵感，你就可以记住所有细节。

关于“记忆电影”的几个创意

如果你对亨利八世的这几位妻子有一些了解，例如，你知道阿拉贡的凯瑟琳是西班牙人，你就可以利用这个信息制作电影。你可以想象阿拉贡的凯瑟琳哀伤地乘坐雄伟的西班牙大帆船，沿泰晤士河而下缓缓离去。而站在河对岸的安妮·博林则是一脸严肃地把头高高扬起，看着站在前方的民众。如果你对这几位夫人所知不多，你也可以打趣她们的名字一番。比如，因为珍·西摩死去了，可以用“真死了，没有了”来记忆。

那么克里维斯的安妮呢？你对她有什么了解？她因为长得丑而出名，亨利八世在离婚时，给了她一大笔赡养费。你不妨想象一下，一位穿着奢华的丑女人，舒服地坐在一大堆金币上。

那么，另外两位凯瑟琳——霍华德和帕尔呢？你除了知道她们其中有一位被处死、另一位存活下来以外，对她们的了解并不多。对于凯瑟琳·霍华德，你可以在她的姓氏霍华德上做文章，想象亨利八世在砍掉她头的时候想着“活不得（霍华德）！”。至于凯瑟琳·帕尔，你可以记住她的姓氏帕尔（Parr）与聚会（party）谐音，因为她在亨利八世去世后还可以参加派对——想象她开心跳舞的模样。

神奇的大脑

世界冠军

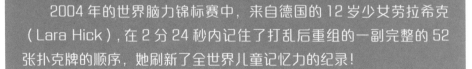

2004 年的世界脑力锦标赛中，来自德国的 12 岁少女劳拉希克（Lara Hick），在 2 分 24 秒内记住了打乱后重组的一副完整的 52 张扑克牌的顺序，她刷新了全世界儿童记忆力的纪录！

迷你记忆工具

押韵、文字游戏、歌曲等都是很好的迷你记忆工具，能够帮助你记住一些很枯燥的东西，诸如一串文字清单或者语法之类。除此之外，你也有足够的理由与记忆力玩耍，因为在学习事物的过程中，你越感到开心，就越容易记住事物。

★ 押韵。使用押韵可以让某些事件在你的记忆中根深蒂固，例如有名的“1666 年伦敦那场大火就像在烧腐烂的木头（In 1666 London burnt like rotten stick）”或是“1492 年哥伦布航行在蓝色的大海上（In 1492 Columbus sailed the ocean blue）”。

★ 文字游戏。如果你必须用外文记住一个很陌生的名字或词语，试着看看有没有可能玩一下文字游戏。例如你发现，法文的 sur 是“在……上面”的意思，sous 则表示“在……下面”的意思，这两个词很容易混淆。你可以这样来记：sur 是 surface（表面）上的 sur，而 sous 则是隐藏在表面之下的（somewhere under the surface）。

★ 歌曲。你是不是觉得很奇怪，为什么利用自己最喜欢的歌曲来记住歌词很容易，但是却很难记住日期、名称或是更复杂的事情？一首好的歌曲包含了节奏、吸引人的旋律，你在聆听的时候很享受，也会想跟着唱起来。记住，当你在把想记住的事物融入旋律中时，千万不要选择不喜欢或者你不太熟悉的歌。举例来说，如果你想记住罗马数字，可以利用下面这首数字歌谣，再搭配上你喜欢的旋律。

"X"代表 10 个玩伴，他们聪明又可爱；

"V"代表 5 个姑娘，她们一起去买菜；

"I"代表我一个人上山去砍柴；

"C"代表 100；

"D"代表 500；

"M"代表 1000 个士兵；

"L"代表 50，虽然它也很无奈！

创建记忆宫殿

你是否有过这种体验，当在做某件事情做到一半的时候忽然分了神，完全忘了自己当初要做什么。一直要等回到起点，才会想起来。为什么会这样呢？这是因为大脑擅长记忆某件事情发生的地点。

你可以运用你的记忆宫殿，将思绪和地点联系在一起。我是从古罗马人那里学到这个方法的——他们是很伟大的发明家，这种叫作“罗马系统”的记忆法就是由他们发明的。不过我更喜欢称其为“宫殿”，就好像在大脑中有一座很豪华的宫殿，可以放很多东西。使用“记忆宫殿”的诀窍，在于你可以把宫殿里所有的东西都放在同一个地方。这表示，你可以记住放在宫殿里的任何事情。这有点像本书第 14 页讨论的衣柜——你把某个信息与某件已知的事情联系在一起。

“记忆宫殿”可以发挥很好的作用，因为它使用你的联想力来记忆。

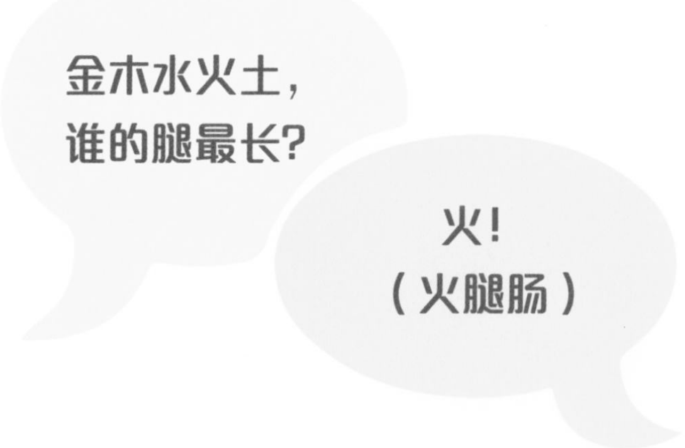

脑力测试

1. 太阳系八大行星的顺序是什么？请你在脑海中回放一次你的记忆电影！

2. 有一个人被问，他的几个女儿长得什么样子。他回答说：“她们中除了两个人以外，其他全都是金发。另外，除了两个人以外，其他全都是褐发，而且除了两个人以外，其他全部是红发。”请问，他有几个女儿？

3. 你看不到它的身体，感受不到它的存在，听不到它的声音，闻不到它的气味。它总是躲在星星后面和山丘的下方，全身上下都是空洞。它是什么？

4. 六个玻璃杯排成一排，前三个杯子里装满了果汁，后三个杯子是空的。如果只能移动一只玻璃杯的话，你能让三个装果汁的杯子与三个空杯子交错排列吗？

答案：

1. 水星、金星、地球、火星、木星、土星、天王星、海王星。
2. 三个，一个金发、一个褐发、一个红发。
3. 黑暗。
4. 可以把第二个玻璃杯中的果汁倒进第五个空玻璃杯中。

属于你的记忆宫殿

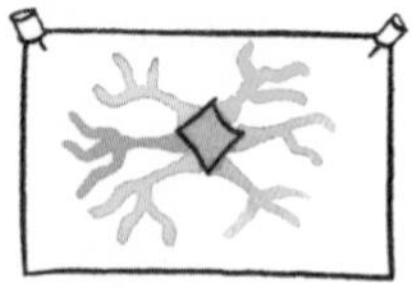

首先，运用你的想象力，让记忆宫殿发挥作用。请你多花点时间和精力来做这件事，并通过绘制思维导图来帮助自己。如此一来，你就会知道宫殿里的每个房间里都有什么东西，也可以清晰地看到它们的摆放顺序。

现在，当你走进记忆宫殿时，首先映入眼帘的是什么？是一道宽敞光亮的白色大理石阶梯，一直向上延伸至二楼。请把这道阶梯加进你的思维导图。然后，观察一下，你还看到了什么？天花板上是不是有一盏闪闪发亮的水晶吊灯？它不停地闪烁着，光影浮动。角落里是不是有个巨大的古董老爷钟，正在滴答作响？那么，请你把它们都加进到思维导图中去。最后，看看脚下，你正站在什么地方？一块镶着黄色长条流苏的天蓝色地毯？动一动你的脚趾头，感受一下地毯的柔软。等你清楚地知道大厅里所有的摆设之后，请你走进下一个房间。这里是哪里？会客室吗？你打量一下四周，第一眼看到的是——一个漂亮的鱼缸，里面有很多亮红色的金鱼游来游去……

请充分运用你的想象力和感官，直到整个宫殿的样子在你的脑海中变得越来越清晰。

记住，你必须多次使用思维导图，才可以将这些事物装入记忆中去。思维导图帮助你把信息储存在记忆宫殿中，并且帮你记住宫殿中所有的东西。如果你愿意的话，你完全可以按照自己家的样子来打造记忆宫殿。

启动记忆宫殿

假设你必须记住下面清单上所列的全部事情：

- ★ 遛狗
- ★ 游戏机
- ★ 足球
- ★ 照相机
- ★ 午餐盒
- ★ 手机
- ★ 地理作业
- ★ 清理鱼缸
- ★ 新买的 CD
- ★ 帮妈妈浇花

现在，你是否对你的记忆宫殿有了更清楚的了解？请记住，让想象力尽情驰骋！

首先，需要记住的是遛狗。想象你的狗在白色大理石阶梯上面跑上跑下。它兴奋地呜呜叫，拼命地摇尾巴，嘴里叼着牵引绳跑来跑去时，爪子在阶梯上发出“咔哒咔哒”的声音。

然后你在房子里面看到了什么？水晶吊灯？而你需要记住的事情是——对了，是游戏机。应该怎样把水晶吊灯和游戏机联系在一起呢？你可以想象游戏机变成了一个人，然后像一只猫一样跳到吊灯上面，发出“叮叮咚咚”的声音。你可以看到水晶吊灯随着游戏机的电线来回晃个不停。

下一个你要记住的是足球。它看起来是什么样子的？你可以想象它是一个闪着白光、用平滑皮革做成的球。请你在想象的场景中嗅一下它皮革的味道。你把它丢在天蓝色的地毯上，重复丢几次，然后用地毯将它包住卷起来，像极了一块超级大的甜软馅饼。

接下来，我们需要记住的是照相机。看一看，在你的宫殿里还有什么？哦，对，那座老爷钟。你可以想象着打开老爷钟，把照相机挂到它的钟摆上。于是，你可以看到钟摆左右摆动，听到时钟发出滴答声，以及照相机随着钟摆打到钟箱壁时发出的声音。

给你的练习

现在，轮到你来试一试了。请你继续记忆剩下的六件事情，发挥想象力，将它们与宫殿里的其他东西联想起来，尽可能在这些东西之间创造出关联性。

数字—形状法

除了“电影记忆法”“记忆宫殿”，另外两个记忆工具分别是“数字—形状法”与“数字—韵律法”。后两者都是把数字作为记忆的根据——与记忆宫殿有些类似。如同记忆宫殿一样，当你希望记住某个信息的时候，只需要把想记住的事情与数字联想在一起，就可以把它们全部记住了，简单易行。让我们先从“数字—形状法”开始吧。与其他记忆工具一样，这个方法之所以非常有用，是因为它也运用了想象力与联想力。

记住形状很有用

请看下一页的图表及其对应的数字。你是否可以看出每个图案的形状都像一个数字？请你花点时间研究一下，并指出这些图案代表哪些数字。请你为每个数字绘制一幅有大纲主干的思维导图，在每条主干上分别写下它们代表哪个数字，然后在次分支上画出图案。持续不断地运用你的思维导图，把每个数字与它的图案联系在一起。

接下来，不断地练习数字—形状法。你的电话号码是多少？用数字—形状法把它们写下来。你的生日是哪一天？也请用数字—形状法写下来。当你熟悉了这种方法以后，可以利用它来记忆任何事情，特别是：

★ 清单上面按顺序排列的所有事情；
★ 每个人的生日；
★ 你在哪一天做了什么特别的事情；
★ 历史上的大事件发生在哪一年；
★ 电话号码——以防哪天手机丢了；
★ 事情发生的时间，例如喜欢的电影几点开场，比赛、课程几点开始。

0 甜甜圈

1 画笔

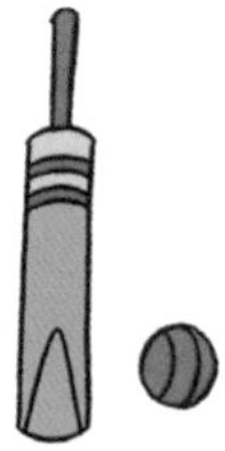

10 球棒与球

2 天鹅

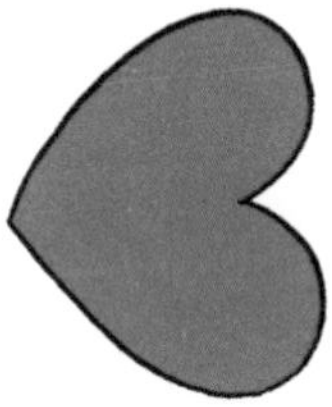

3 爱心

4 帆船

5 钩子

6 象鼻

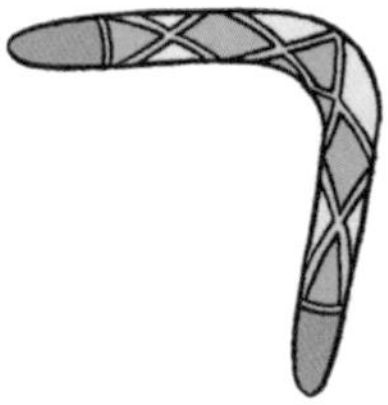

7 飞去来器

8 雪人

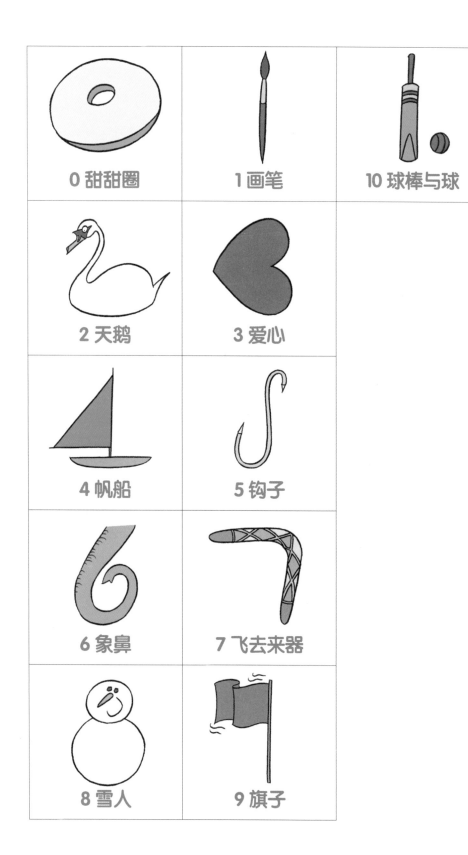

9 旗子

现在，到了玩数字游戏的时间了。请你按顺序记住以下列表中的词汇：

0 喂金鱼
1 滑板
2 比萨
3 棒球帽
4 钥匙
5 CD
6 背包
7 足球鞋
8 家庭作业
9 给爷爷的礼物
10 洗澡

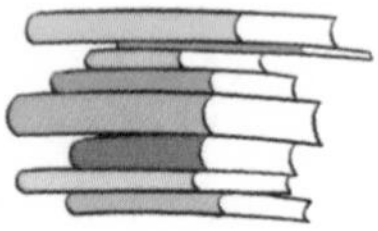

加速你的想象力，在大脑中描绘一幅画面，将列表中的所有词汇都联系起来。你会惊讶地发现，把这些词汇的顺序全部记住原来如此容易。下面，就让我们看看，应该如何把这些词汇跟数字图案联系在一起。

0 喂金鱼。你可以想象把好几百个甜甜圈丢进超级大的鱼缸里，然后鱼儿们一拥而上，狼吞虎咽地把甜甜圈吃掉。

1 滑板。不妨想象你的好朋友丹正站在滑板上，他一边挥舞着巨大的画笔，一边在地上喷洒五颜六色的油漆，从小丘上面滑下来。

2 比萨。想象河面上有一大群美丽的白天鹅，它们正在争抢一大块漂浮在水上的比萨。

3 棒球帽。你可以想象一顶红色的棒球帽，帽舌上面很多爱心图案。

4 钥匙。想象自己正站在一艘漂亮的、闪闪发光的崭新帆船上面。你把船锚抛到海里，但它其实不是锚，而是一把巨大的金钥匙。

5 CD。想象自己把一张闪亮的CD向空中高高抛起，等它落下来掉到一个光滑的金属钩子上时发出了刺耳的声音。

6 背包。你可以想象一只大象用象鼻卷起你的背包，缓缓地在附近的大街闲逛，它一边闲逛还一边得意洋洋地大吼着。

7 足球鞋。你可以想象自己丢出一支七彩的飞去来器，等它飞回来的时候，它的两边竟然各自吊着一双沾满泥巴、湿乎乎的足球鞋。

8 家庭作业。想象你在后院堆了一个很大的雪人，它的眼睛是用木炭做的，鼻子是用胡萝卜做的。你让它替你写家庭作业。

9 给爷爷的礼物。你不妨想象，爷爷把一杆旗子插在一个又大又引人注目的礼物上面，旗子随风不停地飘扬着。

10 洗澡。想象你用球棒把球打进一缸热腾腾的泡泡浴里。当球掉进水里时，发出很大的声音，溅得你一身都是暖暖的、有着甜香气味的肥皂泡。

一遍遍地练习吧，如果你重复练习多次，就可以永远地记住这些事情。

数字—韵律法

“数字—韵律法”与“数字—形状法”很类似，但这种方法并不需要将数字与它的形状联系起来，而是要把数字与它的韵脚联系起来。你可以尝试用这个方法记忆同类型的事物。

以下面几个数字的英文读法为例，请你分别将它们的英文大声读出来。

 0（zero）——英雄（hero）	 5（five）——蜂巢（hive）	 10（ten）——母鸡（hen）
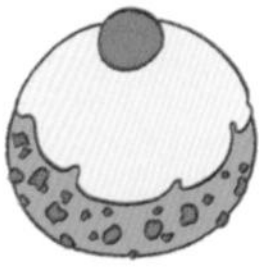 1（one）——圆面包（bun）	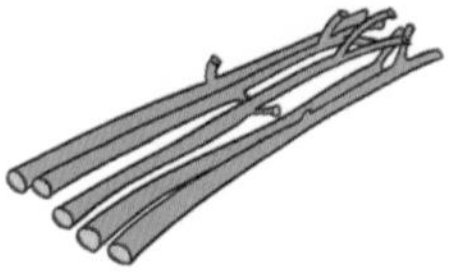 6（six）——木棍（sticks）	
 2（two）——鞋子（shoe）	 7（seven）——天堂（heaven）	
 3（three）——树（tree）	 8（eight）——溜冰鞋（skate）	
 4（four）——门（door）	 9（nine）——葡萄藤（vine）	

与之前使用“数字一形状法”一样，请你重复练习几次，并且绘制一幅简单的思维导图来记住它们。然后请你把书合起来，回忆一下哪个词语与数字 4（four）押韵？是门（door）！哪个词语与数字 8（eight）押韵？是溜冰鞋（skate）！你看，就是这么简单！

现在，请你用已经记住的数字（例如你的电话号码）来练习“数字一韵律法”。举例来说，英雄（hero），鞋子（shoe），英雄（hero），溜冰鞋（skate），木棍（sticks），溜冰鞋（skate），木棍（sticks），门（door），蜂巢（hive），鞋子（shoe），树（tree），就是 02086864523。

什么东西落下来
却不会摔碎？

夜幕。

神奇的大脑
关于鱼类的一些事实

你有没有听说过金鱼只拥有 3 秒的记忆？事实上，人类低估了这群全身长满鳞片的动物朋友。英国朴利茅斯大学的科学家发现，金鱼的记忆力可以持续 3 个月，它们甚至能够记住时间。研究小组训练金鱼在每天特定的时间吃东西，他们在鱼缸里放了杠杆，金鱼只有记住特定的时间并且想办法压下杠杆，才能吃到东西。

当你了解到“数字—韵律法”的使用诀窍以后，让我们来看看，你是否能够用这些方法记住以下顺序的词汇：

0 窗户（Window）
1 椅子（Chair）
2 花朵（Flower）
3 小鸟（Bird）
4 漫画书（Comic book）
5 獾（Badger）
6 照片（Picture）
7 床（Bed）
8 肥皂（Soap）
9 橘子（Orange）
10 足球（Football）

如果你想按顺序记住这些词汇，只要把这些词汇与它们对应数字的韵脚通过强有力的方法联系在一起。没错，这个强有力的方法就是联想力和想象力。

把 8 分成两半，
是多少？

两个 0！

0——英雄——窗户

请你想象一位正在救人的英雄，他满身肌肉，紧握拳头，咬紧牙关，冲破窗户去帮你打败敌人。你听到了窗户碰撞的声音，以及英雄为了救你而与敌人奋战时用力挥拳发出的怒吼声。

现在，你要施展想象的魔法，把英雄和窗户这两个词联系在一起。在脑海中对英雄打破窗户产生强烈的视觉印象，并运用感官让这个印象在心中根深蒂固。因为英雄（hero）和0（zero）的韵脚相似（英文发音），所以你只需要记住英雄和窗户之间的关系，就可以记住0（zero）和窗户之间的关系了。怎么样，很简单吧！

现在，让我们看看如何把其他几个数字与记忆对象联系在一起。

1——圆面包——椅子

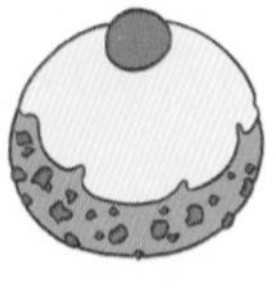

想象一块巨大的圆面包放在一张摇摇欲坠的椅子上。这块圆面包太重了，结果把椅子腿压断了！想象自己闻到了新鲜的面包香味，尝尝它的味道，好吃极了！

2——鞋子——花朵

想象你最喜欢的一双鞋子上长出了一株亮红色的鲜花。你想把它摘下来，可是它的茎毛茸茸的，弄得你的手指很痒。

3——树——小鸟

想象一棵很高的树，上面立着一只漂亮的黄色小鸟。那只小鸟唱着你从没听过的节奏欢快的歌。你在树下跟着小鸟唱歌的节奏跳起舞来，觉得自己是世界上最快乐的人！

4——门——漫画书

想象卧室的门是用你最喜欢的漫画书的彩页制作的。请你想想漫画书里的各种角色在书页间跑来跑去，而且当你开门的时候，还可以听到书页沙沙作响的声音。

5——蜂窝——獾

想象一只獾，正在用它的鼻子嗅着一个蜂窝。不过，这只獾身上的毛不是黑白条纹的，而像蜜蜂一样是黑黄条纹的。你可以想象蜂蜜从它的爪子流到了它的毛上。用你的手沾一沾黏黏的蜂蜜，尝一尝它甜甜的味道。

6——木棍——照片

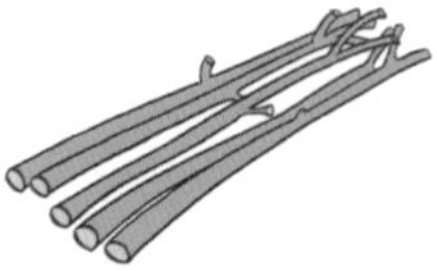

想象自己用四根光滑的木棍，将你最喜欢的全家福照片装裱起来。

7——天堂——床

想象天堂里的所有天使正香甜地睡在一张宽大、洁白、柔软的床上。

8——溜冰鞋——肥皂

想象你正在溜冰，但你脚上穿的不是溜冰鞋，而是两块捆在一起的粉红色肥皂！当你把画面拉近的时候，还可以看到在你身后的地板上，留下两行肥皂泡的痕迹。

9——葡萄藤——橘子

想象一株巨大的弯弯曲曲的葡萄藤，就像《杰克与豌豆》里杰克的那棵豌豆树。不过，这株葡萄藤上长出的不是葡萄，而是多汁的橘子。

10——母鸡——足球

想象一只蹲在窝里下蛋的母鸡，但是它下的不是鸡蛋，而是一个个黑白相间的足球。

经过几次练习以后，你每次都有可能记住 11 组联想。很快你就会发现，这种方法可以灵活使用，以达到不同的记忆目的。例如，如果把记忆对象由一串词汇换成一串数字，你只需要记住韵律相近的词汇即可：圆面包（bun）等于 1（one），鞋子（shoe）等于 2（two），树（tree）等于 3（three）！你会发现通过韵律进行记忆比直接记忆数字要高效得多。

让你的记忆量倍增

你可以同时利用两种数字记忆法，帮助自己记住两倍的信息。例如，现在你必须要记住两份不同的列表，你可以使用“数字一形状法”记住一份，然后用“数字一韵律法”记住另一份。

记忆的魔力

你有没有在 2004 年英国 BBC 电视台播出的儿童节目中看过我的表演？节目组要求我在节目里观察一个射飞镖的靶子。藏在每个数字后面的图案都与节目有关。我有几分钟的时间来记住这些图案，然后所有的图案都被盖起来。在节目进行到尾声时，他们会测试我是否仍然记得。你问我怕不怕？我当然不怕了。我觉得好玩极了！我利用了“数字一形状法”记住了所有内容，而且全部正确地回答出来。现在，你也可以跟我一样。

脑力训练

请你明天早上起床以后，在纸上写下 5 个词汇，然后给自己 1 分钟的时间，利用“数字一形状法”或“数字一韵律法”来记住这串词汇。接下来，把这张纸放在口袋里，你开始做别的事。

吃午餐的时候，请你再想想这串词汇是什么。你还记得这 5 个词汇以及它们的顺序吗？如果忘记了，请你重新再记忆一次，并加深数字与数字之间的联想力，请把纸重新放回口袋，并在晚餐之前再测试。

你还能够完全记得它们吗？真是太棒了！下一次，请尝试在 1 分钟之内记住 10 个词汇，然后可以不断增加每次的记忆量……

恭喜你，现在你已经学会 5 种主要的记忆工具了——思维导图、记忆电影、记忆宫殿以及两种数字记忆法。你需要通过坚持不懈的练习，才能让这些方法变成一种本能习惯。经过不断的练习，你可以很快记住你想要记住的任何事情。现在，我们要把所有的记忆工具整合起来，让你的记忆力大显身手！

有一头猪，它走啊走啊，走到了英国，结果它变成了什么？

Pig！

用汉语拼音记忆数字①

“数字一韵律法”是最有效、最简易、最成功的记忆方法之一，它改变了你的学习观念，你是不是曾经觉得自己的记忆力差极了？而现在，你或许会惊讶于自己竟然拥有和记忆大师一样的记忆力！

但是，在学习这种方法的过程中，你或许会遇到一只“拦路虎”：将数字转换为英文单词，再联系韵律相似的单词，最后再转为中文词语。问题就出在英文单词的转换上，这需要学习者具有一定的英语学习基础，而对于大多数中国小读者来说，则存在一定的难度。

0～10 数字中文代码		
0	líng	铃儿、零钱 
1	yī	医生、衣服 
2	èr	耳朵 
3	sān	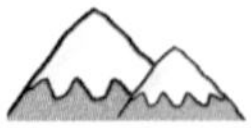 山、扇子、杉树
4	sì	寺庙、司机
5	wǔ	武术、舞蹈 
6	liù	溜溜球、柳树 
7	qī	妻子、气球、棋子 
8	bā	巴士、芭蕉
9	jiǔ	酒、舅舅
10	shí	石头、食物 

①本节的记忆法案例由本书译者、世界思维导图锦标赛冠军刘艳女士提供。

因此，为了使记忆方法更适合你的思维习惯，我们可以将英语单词换为自己熟悉的汉语拼音。上一页中分享的一套记忆方法，是我根据韵母相同或读音相近的汉语拼音所编写的，希望你在进行联想练习时可作为参考。

当有了一套自己的“数字一韵律法”之后，你就可以用自己最习惯的思维方式来记忆数字串了。是不是跃跃欲试了呢？快与老师和小伙伴们一起交流学习心得吧！

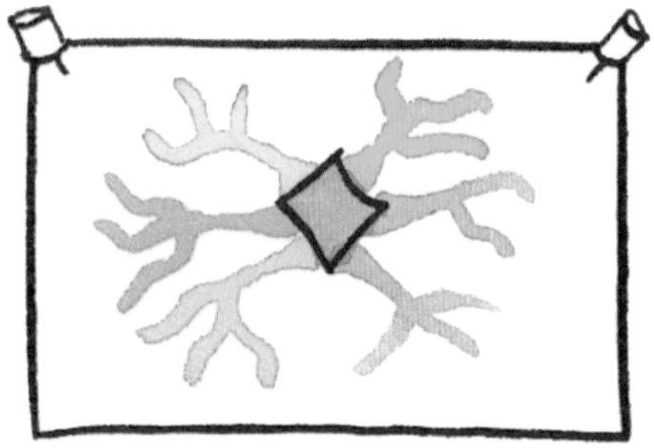

第五章

秀出你的记忆力

无论你想记住什么，无论它多么简单或多么复杂，本书提供的记忆工具都可以帮助你达到目的。

“你说什么？任何想记住的事情？”没错，你可以记住任何你想记住的事情。

只要运用大脑不到 1% 的空间，就可以记住所有想记住的事情！

关于记忆，你学习得越多，练习得越勤，大脑就“记忆”得越发娴熟，你就越能轻松地记住更多事情。所以，无论是历史上百位名人的详细资料，还是朋友们的生日，你都有办法轻松记住。那么就让我们来看看，日常生活中你需要记住的事情通常有哪几类。

记忆日常小事

你每天需要记住一大堆小事、杂事，所以总是很容易忘记。例如：

★ 班上新同学的名字；
★ 球队比赛的分数；
★ 各种清单（例如假期要带的东西，或是购物清单）；
★ 电话号码；
★ 需要随身携带的物品（例如钥匙、运动服等）；
★ 外语书中的语法规则。

有了记忆工具以后，你就再也不会忘记上述这些小事了。你会发现思维导图、记忆电影、记忆宫殿以及数字记忆法都是非常有效的快速记忆工具。现在，就试着开动你的大脑，让它开始记忆吧！

与你的记忆力玩耍

有许多非常神奇的游戏能让你的“记忆肌肉”得到充分锻炼，例如“Kim’s Game”“Pairs and Auntie Sal”（两款英语记忆游戏）。不过，这些都是聪明人发明的众多游戏中的冰山一角。举例来说，下棋也是全世界的天才们都很喜欢的游戏，同时也是绝佳的记忆力辅助工具。而找词游戏、填字游戏、大家来找茬等益智小游戏同样也可以让你的“记忆肌肉”得到充分的锻炼。

脑力测试

1. 你需要重复几次，才能永远记住一件事情？

2. 如果你想记住某件事，中间需要间隔多久重复记忆一次？

3. 休息是否能够帮助记忆？为什么？

4. 你应该每隔多久休息一次？一次可以休息多久？

答案：

1. 5次。

2. 第一次，10分钟以后；第二次，1天后；第三次，1周后；第四次，3~6个月后。

3. 休息可以帮助你把学习中段过程缩短，而那段时间正是你最不容易集中注意力的时候。

4. 每隔45分钟休息5~10分钟。

记人名游戏

记住人名的最好方法就是发挥你的想象力。例如，你可以通过记住对方的长相或类似的其他有趣方法，把你想记住的那个人的名字拿来搞怪一下。有些人的名字一模一样，你可以把他们的名字归在同一类，为他们制作一部小型的记忆电影。当人们第一次告诉你他们的名字时，你可以大声地念出来，这样也有助于记忆。

如何才能记住这些人的名字

★ 罗茜（Rosie）——班上新来的一个害羞的女孩

★ 拉斐尔（Raphael）——某个朋友的表兄弟，是从墨西哥城来旅游的

★ 哈利（Harry）——你弟弟新交的性格有点儿古怪的朋友

★ 斯托巴特太太（Mrs Stobbart）——学校新来的老师

★ 戴夫与梅尔（Dave and Mel）——你父母的朋友

如果你想记住罗茜（Rosie）这个名字，你可以想象一朵粉红色的玫瑰（rose）出现在教室门口。如果你想记住拉斐尔的名字，你也可以想象他是位天使（拉斐尔是宗教传统之中的四大天使长之一），从墨西哥城飞到你们这里来了。

至于其他人的名字，用什么方法比较好记呢？你可以试着想想看。

用椰子和木瓜打脑袋，
哪一个比较痛？

脑袋比较痛！

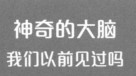

神奇的大脑
我们以前见过吗

来自德国的 12 岁少女卡特瑞纳·邦克（Katharina Bunk）是 2003 年世界脑力锦标赛儿童组的冠军获得者。在那一年的比赛中，她只花了 15 分钟就记住了 90 个人的名字和长相。

分数的战争

一场精彩球赛结束几天以后，你可能还能记得当天的比赛成绩。但过了几个星期以后，你还能在与队友讨论时，记起球队整个赛季的分数吗?

书中介绍的几种方法都可以帮助你记住每场球赛的分数，例如数字记忆法，此外，思维导图也能帮你不断记忆球赛的分数。

如果你必须记住世界杯某几场比赛的分数：

巴西：西班牙——2 ：1

爱尔兰：俄罗斯——1 ：1

英格兰：德国——3 ：2

中国：俄罗斯——2 ：1

请你选用一种数字记忆法将每场比赛的分数与国家联系在一起，然后绘制一幅思维导图。以下是你运用“数字—韵律法”记住的第一场球赛的分数：

关于巴西对西班牙这场球赛，比分是 2 ：1（鞋子与圆面包）。你可以想象一双很大的黄色球鞋（巴西队球衣是黄色的）正在踢一个超级大的圆面包，而这个圆面包的形状很像西班牙地图。你还可以想象那双球鞋每踢一次，就踢得满地都是小圆面包的碎屑。

至于爱尔兰对俄罗斯那场球赛的比分是 1 ： 1（圆面包与圆面包）。你可以想象两个很大的圆面包，头顶着头想把对方摔倒。其中一个圆面包是亮绿色的，而且头上还沾上了一株三叶草（爱尔兰的国花）；另一个圆面包则是紫色的，形状很像甜菜根——因为俄罗斯人最喜欢喝甜菜汤。

现在，请你想想，记住其他比分应该怎么玩呢？

记忆清单的乐趣

你可以将记忆清单想象成一个有趣的游戏，游戏的过程中记住所有与朋友、家人有关的事情。举例来说，你的家人正在准备一次长途旅行，关于要带的物品拟定了一份清单。如果这份清单很长，可以采用记忆工具来帮助记忆，最适合的莫过于电影记忆法和记忆宫殿了。

让我们先从电影记忆法开始。想象你的姨妈正在准备一次长途旅行。她正想着应该往背包里放些什么，而你在一旁帮忙。你挑的每件东西都是她用得到的，不过在她打包行李之前，你必须记得背包里面都有些什么。做这件事情的时候，请录制你的记忆电影，记住背包里的全部东西。想象以下是你建议她带上的东西：

1. 驱蚊水
2. 遮阳帽
3. 人字拖
4. 泳衣
5. 沙滩浴巾
6. 一本好书
7. 睡衣
8. 牙刷

录制记忆电影

萨尔姨妈去蒙古

想象你独自一人走在丛林里，突然间你被一大群嗡嗡叫的蚊子包围——你甚至可以听到它们高频率的嗡嗡声充斥在四周。驱蚊水在哪里？

快拿出来！快点喷！你往前走了一会，来到了一块阳光普照的空地，你可以感觉到温暖的阳光照在后颈。

你马上戴了遮阳帽，然后你突然发觉脚趾头被鞋子磨伤了。好痛！检查过后，你发现脚趾头磨出了烦人的水泡。不过不用担心！因为你马上可以换上舒服的人字拖！

现在你觉得有点热了，出了点汗，不过马上就能凉快一下了——眼前出现一个很棒的瀑布，瀑布倾泻而下形成天然的岩石游泳池，蓝色的池水，看上去清凉极了。你很快换上泳衣，然后跳进池子里。

凉爽的池水出乎你的意料，于是你开始在泳池里游起来。你游了一会，重新振作精神，然后从水里爬出来，拿出沙滩浴巾擦干身体，感受到浴巾柔软的触感。这时候你整个人神清气爽，而且很放松，于是你拿出一本很棒的书来看。

等你走回帐篷时，突然感觉非常想睡觉，并且开始打哈欠、伸懒腰。是该睡觉的时间了！于是你换上睡衣，拿起牙刷朝浴室走去。

整理运用记忆宫殿

你是否想试试利用记忆宫殿来记住前一页中萨尔姨妈的所有行李？如果你的脑海中已经为记忆宫殿描绘出了一幅清晰的图片，那就太好了！如果还没有，请你快速浏览一下自己所绘制的思维导图，为记忆注入活力！

现在，请你从以下清单中所列的第一个物品开始，运用想象力将其与你的记忆宫殿联系起来。然后，请你一直做下去，直到把清单上的所有物品都放进记忆宫殿为止。

1. 蛙鞋
2. CD 播放器
3. 防晒霜
4. 笑话集
5. 照相机
6. 沙滩浴巾
7. 洗发水
8. 写生簿
9. 电池
10. 发夹

神奇的大脑

你知道候鸟有着绝佳的长期记忆力吗？每年大约有 5000 万只候鸟飞回它们原来生长的地方过冬。有些鸟的远距离飞行更为惊人，例如北极燕鸥，可以飞至 1 万千米甚至更远。它们为了找到回家的路，会根据太阳、月亮、行星的位置在体内设置“罗盘”。同时，它们还会借助地球磁场的指引找到方向。有些候鸟甚至会利用其绝佳的嗅觉到达目的地。

如果你想记住清单上所列的所有物品，可以按照下面的方法来做：

蛙鞋。想象你穿着蛙鞋，在记忆宫殿里的一道很长的白色大理石阶梯上来回地走。你听见自己每走一步，脚下的鞋就发出一种怪声。

CD 播放器。想象记忆宫殿里的水晶灯吊的不是水晶，而是 CD。看着这些 CD 在晃动的时候反射出灼眼的亮光来。

现在，开始自由想象吧！

腿骨对脚说了什么？

只要跟着我，你就可以走到任何地方。

扩充你的记忆容量

现在，你已经对记忆少量的信息驾轻就熟了，但如何记住更复杂的事情呢？例如：

★ 一出戏剧中重要角色的所有台词；
★ 为了演戏需要记住的外语对话；
★ 你正在读的书里的剧情与人物；
★ 昨天晚上做的梦；
★ 英国所有国王与王后的名字；
★ 科学或者地理实验的复杂过程；
★ 配合你最喜欢的曲调的舞步；
★ 某种游戏或者运动的比赛规则；
★ 班上每个同学的生日和年龄。

最棒的记忆工具——思维导图，可以助你一臂之力，通常情况下，结合电影记忆法和数字记忆法一起使用效果更佳。现在就请你使用这些记忆工具来激活大脑，秀出你的记忆力吧！

神奇的大脑

2004 年，来自奥地利 16 岁的约阿希姆 · 泰勒（Joachim Thaler）在 5 分钟之内，记住了随机选出来的 44 个历史事件的日期。这通常是一名学生在 1 年之内才能记住的日期数量。够厉害吧？

脑力测试

在蒙古的丛林里，萨尔姨妈一早醒来，感觉在睡衣口袋里好像有什么东西。这个东西有头有尾，但是没有脚。当萨尔姨妈起床时，感觉这个东西在口袋里动来动去。不过这件事并没有吓到她，她还是像平常一样去做早餐。请问为什么她这样镇定？

答案：

因为她知道那是一枚硬币。【英文里硬币的正面与反面被称为"head"（头）和"tail"（尾）。】

如何记住生日和年龄

假设你们班一共有 20 名学生，无论是谁过生日，都会买一个大蛋糕并点上蜡烛大家一起庆祝。身为班长的你，必须负责在每个同学生日的那一天，去买一个大蛋糕。所以你必须记住每个人的生日时间，你能记得住所有人的生日吗？这太简单了！只要使用思维导图，一切都可以搞定！

你可以采取好几种方式来绘制这幅思维导图：用 12 个大纲主干来代表一年中的 12 个月份，然后在 12 个大纲主干上再添加内容分支，代表在那个月过生日的小寿星；或者，你可以根据同学名字的首字母进行顺序的排列。无论选用哪种方式，你都会发现使用思维导图来记忆同学们的生日和年龄，真的是太简单了。

假设以下是你班上同学的生日名单。请你为它绘制一幅思维导图，如此一来你就可以轻松记住全班同学的生日了。当然，你也可以对此做一次真实的调查和统计，然后使用“数字一韵律法”或者其他记忆方法来记住班上同学的生日。

1. 安于姆，2 月 22 日
2. 安娜，6 月 3 日
3. 本，5 月 27 日
4. 查理，6 月 3 日
5. 戴夫，11 月 4 日
6. 艾莉，11 月 30 日
7. 菲力克斯，12 月 3 日
8. 乔治，3 月 13 日
9. 哈米斯，9 月 5 日
10. 艾瑞丝，10 月 23 日
11. 凯伦，1 月 4 日
12. 米利，7 月 3 日
13. 诺亚，8 月 19 日

14. 奥莉薇亚，1 月 16 日
15. 奥利娅，11 月 1 日
16. 保罗，3 月 8 日
17. 里基，6 月 17 日
18. 史黛丝，9 月 24 日
19. 汤姆，12 月 24 日
20. 维奥莱特，4 月 25 日

神奇的大脑

记忆词语

你玩过这种游戏吗？大家围坐在一起，形成一个圈。首先，选出一位出题者，出题者不直接参与游戏。然后，由出题者任意报出一个名词，比如“大象”。接着，游戏者们按顺时针方向轮流循环进行记忆游戏。每一位游戏者都要按正确的顺序说出前一位游戏者报出的所有名词，并且自己再报出一个新的名词。如果有人报错，就算输掉本轮游戏，游戏即告结束。

你知道玩这个游戏的诀窍吗？尽可能运用想象和联想！将前一位游戏者报出的所有词语用图片或一段剧情串联起来。比如前一位游戏者报出了“大象”“少女”“书”“眼泪”，你就可以把它们串联起来，想象为“大象上坐着一位少女，一边在看书，一边流着眼泪”。联想的时候，注意词语的顺序哦！

“同学们的生日”思维导图

鞋子
汤姆
菲力克斯
门
树
24
3
奥利娅
圆面包
1
戴夫
4
门
艾莉
30
12月
英雄
树
11月
艾瑞丝
鞋子
23
10月
树
同
9月
生
哈米斯
蜂巢
5
24
史黛丝
8月
鞋子
门
7月
19
诺亚
3
圆面包
米利
葡萄
树

们的日
1月
4
凯伦
门
16
奥莉薇亚
圆面包
木棍
2月
22
安于姆
鞋子
鞋子
3月
8
保罗
溜冰鞋
13
乔治
圆面包
树
4月
25
维奥莱特
鞋子
蜂巢
5月
27
杰
鞋子
天堂
6月
3
查理
安娜
树
17
天堂
里基
圆面包

第五章

秀出你的记忆力

如何记住戏剧台词

当你为了演出而必须记住某场戏的台词时，想象你演的这场戏是一部记忆电影。你只要用生动有趣的方法，在大脑中记住你的角色就可以了。请你充分运用自己的感官。假如，你扮演一名非常勇敢的上尉，而此刻一艘海盗船正向海岸逼近，你站在窗边，喊出以下台词：

“雷声与闪电大作！海盗船来了！快点，快点！到城堡的墙边就位！把枪上膛！来人啊，我的剑在哪里？”

请你充分想象自己身临其境的感觉。作为上尉你会说些什么呢？你会感到兴奋、害怕，还是高兴？你有没有办法站着不动？那个时候你的手势是什么？你可以在心里尽可能把台词想象得更生动一点。只要你这么去做，就有可能记住所有的台词，甚至可能演得像好莱坞明星那么棒。如果你想获取更多的帮助，也可以围绕人物角色的动作行为绘制一幅思维导图，并在台词的关键词旁边加一些小图案。

你也可以参考一下台词。请把你要说的、要做的，以及要体验感受的事情记录在你的记忆电影中，然后用一幅思维导图为它们做个总结。第104～105页的思维导图，将告诉你如何才能更巧妙地记住台词。

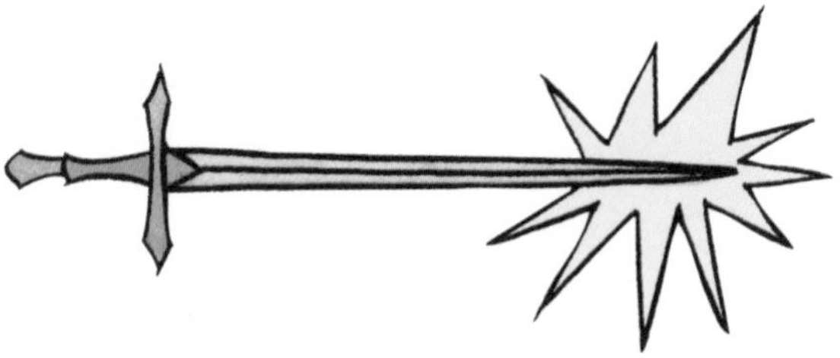

包哈特上尉

（在城堡中）：

雷声与闪电大作！海盗船来了！快点，快点！到城堡的墙边就位！把枪上膛！来人啊，我的剑在哪里?

（侍从递上了剑。）

哦，是的，就是这把剑。这把高贵的剑，是我父亲用西班牙的钢铁，亲手铸造的剑。

（举起这把剑。）

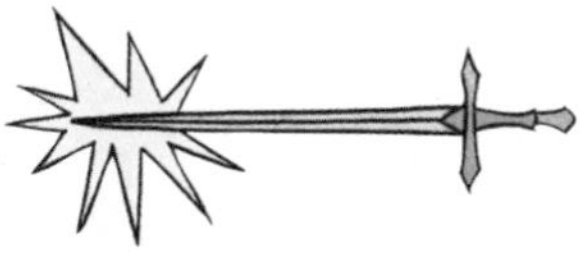

我的剑啊，今天就请你把我带到敌人那里，与他们一决胜负吧！让我为我亲爱的哥哥报仇——他被邪恶的鲍瑞尔谋杀了！

（走进舞台中央的房间，开始表演陷入回忆的模样。）

某天晚上，海盗鲍瑞尔偷偷潜入城堡，抢走了我三位美丽的姐姐。我高贵的哥哥听到声音便冲了出去。他手里紧紧握着剑，与鲍瑞尔厮杀。

（把剑举高，做出决斗的姿势。）

但是鲍瑞尔骗了我哥哥。他说他要投降，我那可怜的哥哥竟然相信了，并准备让他离开，鲍瑞尔趁机突然将剑刺入了我哥哥的心脏。我哥哥因此而丧生，然而鲍瑞尔却逃走了。哦不，怎么会发生这种事！

（身体转向城堡的窗边。）

在用手上的剑刺入仇人的心脏之前，我绝不能悲叹，更不能松懈！鲍瑞尔，我将亲眼见到你死去，因为我——勇敢的上尉包哈特要为哥哥报仇！

（退场。）

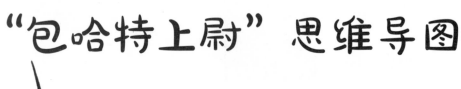

“包哈特上尉”思维导图

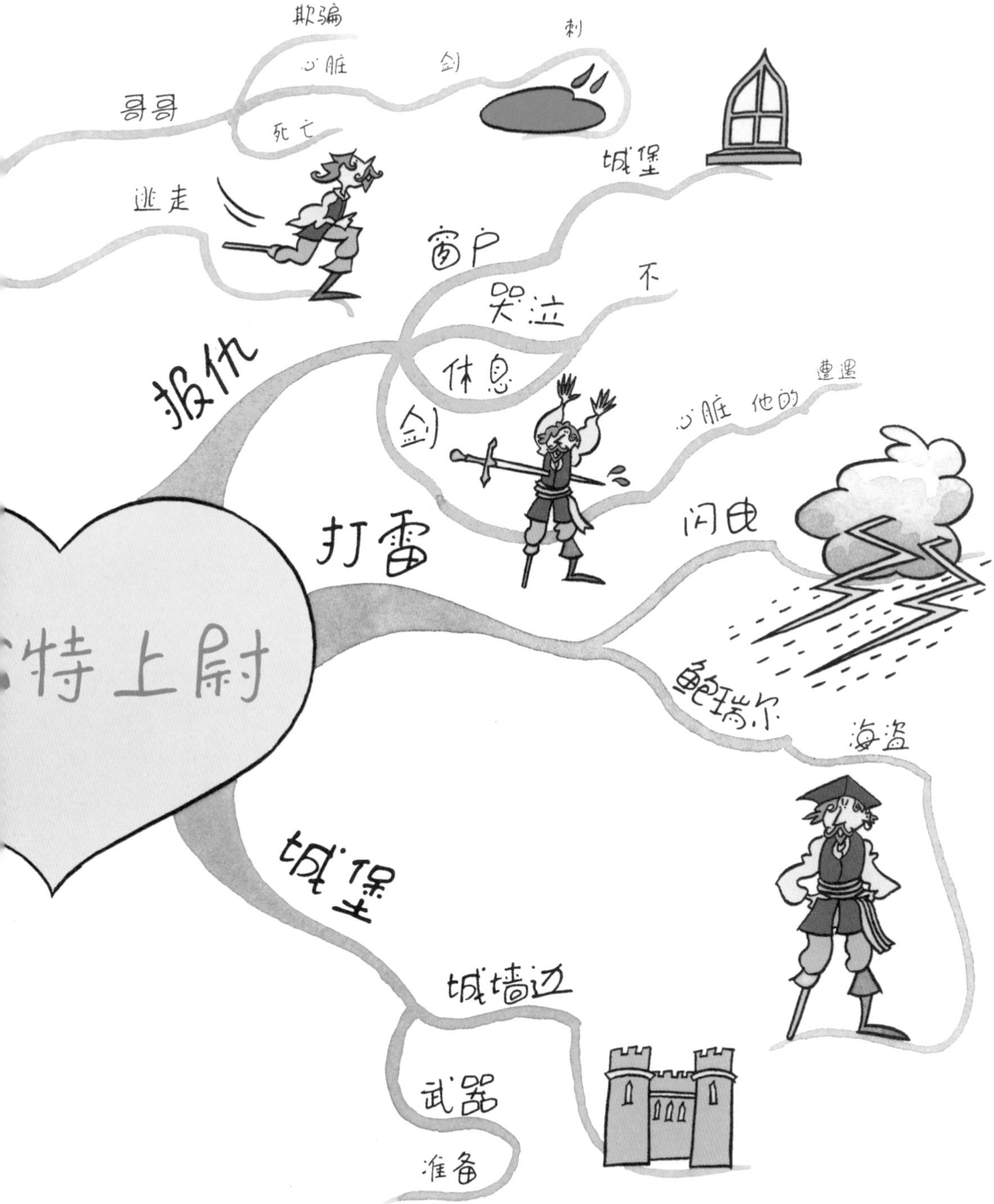
特上尉
报仇
哥哥
欺骗
心脏
剑
刺
死亡
逃走
城堡
窗户
哭泣
不
休息
剑
心脏 他的
遭遇
打雷
闪电
鲍瑞尔
海盗
城堡
城墙边
武器
准备

把人物放进历史里

学历史必须记住很多人名和事件，但是你常常弄不懂它们之间的关系。思维导图能够提供线索，是帮你找出历史人物之间关系的最佳工具。

举个例子，如果你已经学了不少有关英国的历史，你对“征服者”威廉有了一点了解，也知道约克家族的理查与都铎家族的亨利都与玫瑰战争有关。当然，你也知道在法国国王查理四世去世以后，发生了英法百年战争（查理四世在其姐、英国王后伊莎贝拉废黜其丈夫英国国王爱德华二世的事件中扮演了合谋者的角色）。但是你如何将这些事件全部串联在一起呢？思维导图是一个很好的选择，因为它可以帮助你纵览全局，同时更好地记住人物以及事件发生的时间。

英国的国王与女王

请看下一页英国所有国王与女王的在位时间表。然后拿出纸笔准备绘制一幅思维导图。一开始，请你先为每个家族或者氏族画出主要分支。然后再慢慢加上你所知道的国王或者女王的名字，这样能帮助你记住每一个人物。

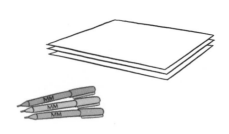

英国的国王与女王

诺曼王朝

威廉一世（征服者） 1066~1087

威廉二世……………… 1087~1100

亨利一世……………… 1100~1135

斯蒂芬………………… 1135~1154

金雀花王朝

亨利二世……………… 1154~1189

理查一世（狮心王） 1189~1199

约翰（失地王）……… 1199~1216

亨利三世……………… 1216~1272

爱德华一世…………… 1272~1307

爱德华二世…………… 1307~1327

爱德华三世…………… 1327~1377

理查二世……………… 1377~1399

兰开斯特王朝

亨利四世……………… 1399~1413

亨利五世……………… 1413~1422

亨利六世……………… 1422~1461

约克王朝

爱德华四世…………… 1461~1483

爱德华五世…………………… 1483

理查三世……………… 1483~1485

都铎王朝

亨利七世……………… 1485~1509

亨利八世……………… 1509~1547

爱德华六世…………… 1547~1553

玛丽一世……………… 1553~1558

伊丽莎白一世………… 1558~1603

斯图亚特王朝

詹姆士一世…………… 1603~1625

查理一世……………… 1625~1649

查理二世……………… 1660~1685

詹姆士二世…………… 1685~1688

威廉三世和玛丽二世………………

1688~1702/1688~1694

安妮…………………… 1702~1714

汉诺威王朝

乔治一世……………… 1714~1727

乔治二世……………… 1727~1760

乔治三世……………… 1760~1820

乔治四世……………… 1820~1830

威廉四世……………… 1830~1837

萨克森－科堡－哥达王朝

维多利亚……………… 1837~1901

爱德华七世…………… 1901~1910

温莎王朝

乔治五世……………… 1910~1936

爱德华八世…………………… 1936

乔治六世……………… 1936~1952

伊丽莎白二世………… 1952~

“英国的国王＆女王”思维导图

的
女王
诺曼王朝
威廉
1
1066~1087
威廉
2
1087~1100
亨利
1
1100~1135
斯蒂芬
1135~1154
金雀花王朝
亨利
2
1154~1189
理查
1
1189~1199
约翰
1199~1216
亨利
3
1216~1272
爱德华
1
1272~1307
爱德华
2
1307~1327
爱德华
3
1327~1377
理查
2
1377~1399
兰开斯特王朝
亨利
4
1399~1413
亨利
5
1413~1422
亨利
6
1422~1461
约克王朝
爱德华
4
1461~1483
爱德华
5
1483
理查
3
1483~1485

捕捉你的梦境

我们每个人晚上都会做梦，只是到了早上不一定都能记得。做梦（包括做白日梦）能使想象力发挥得淋漓尽致。你能够记住的梦越多，对你的想象力就越有帮助，而且还能大大增强你的记忆力。思维导图是捕捉你梦境的最好方法。

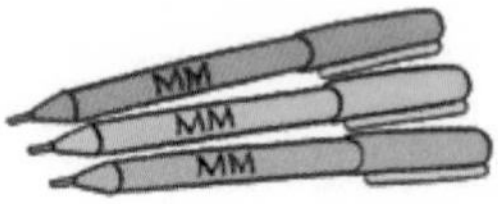

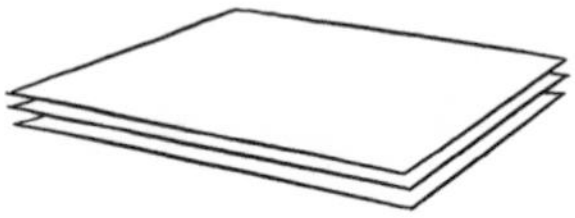

在床边摆几支笔与一个笔记本。当你晚上上床睡觉时，用一两分钟的时间想着做梦这件事情。你不断告诉自己：我会记住我的梦。当你早上起床时，先不要马上从床上爬起来，试着静静地躺一会，让自己保持浅睡眠的状态。用一种舒缓的方式，想象一下大脑里正在想些什么。你的心里是否会出现什么图像或者什么感觉？还是只有几个字？

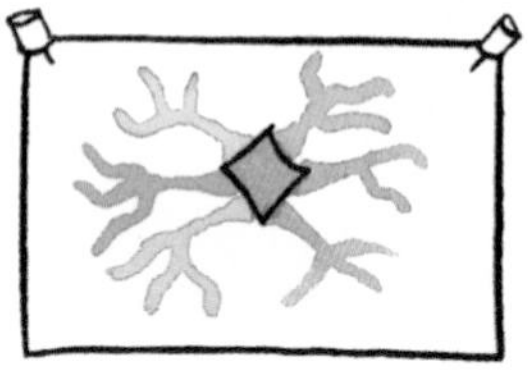

当你躺在床上一动不动时，一些梦境会浮现出来。拿起你的笔记本，将你还记得的梦境绘成一幅思维导图。思维导图有唤醒记忆的强大功能，使用思维导图后你将会发现，你能记住的远比一开始所预期的要多得多。

神奇的大脑

交替使用左右手

你是左撇子还是右撇子？不论你习惯使用左手还是右手，千万不要因为习惯就总是使用某一只手，而很少用另一只手。请你用不常用的那只手来刷牙、梳头发、吃东西或者系鞋带。换一只手来投球或者接球。用你不常用的那只手，或者同时用两只手涂鸦！做任何事情时，请交替使用你的两只手，如此一来，你的左脑和右脑都会变得很发达。

神奇的大脑
改变你的日常习惯

如果你想跟随最喜爱的音乐伴奏学会新的舞步，请你先利用“记忆电影”让你的大脑记住舞步，然后再开始练习舞步，让身体记住它。如果你一开始先让大脑记住了它，那么当你开始练习身体姿势时，就会更轻松地掌握正确的舞步。

将你的梦境描绘成思维导图，看看能否从中找出一个固定的模式。通过对梦的解析你会对自己有更深入的认识。请翻至下一页，看看这幅你也能画得出的思维导图，你能想象这幅图的绘制者，他梦见了什么吗?

想把梦境变为现实，
第一步应该做什么?

起床!

20？
塔
绿色
距离
宫殿
水晶
慢
低
打转
老鹰
等待
小精灵
到达
看
碰撞
着地
招手
醒来
抓住
掠过
头发
下降
潜水
树林
高处
风
快速
上面
我
模糊
飞翔
通过
森林
活着
山谷
感觉
独角兽
山脉
永远
棒
老鹰
狂欢
狂奔
白色
岩石
一起
金黄色
雪
飞走
羽毛
大量
回来
我
柔软
爬
面孔
飞翔
上面
聪明
朝向

“我的梦”思维导图

梦
走廊
安静
长
直
白
亮
形状
移动
随着
我
人们？
说
不
走
下去
门
尽头
巨大
把手
冰冷
闪亮
门
打开
狭窄
石头
黄色
壁架
晴朗
天空
森林
下面
蔚蓝
太阳
气味
树
明亮
顶部
热
土地
巨大
潮湿
鸟
老虎
绿色
猴子
奇异的

掌控记忆力，

收获精彩人生

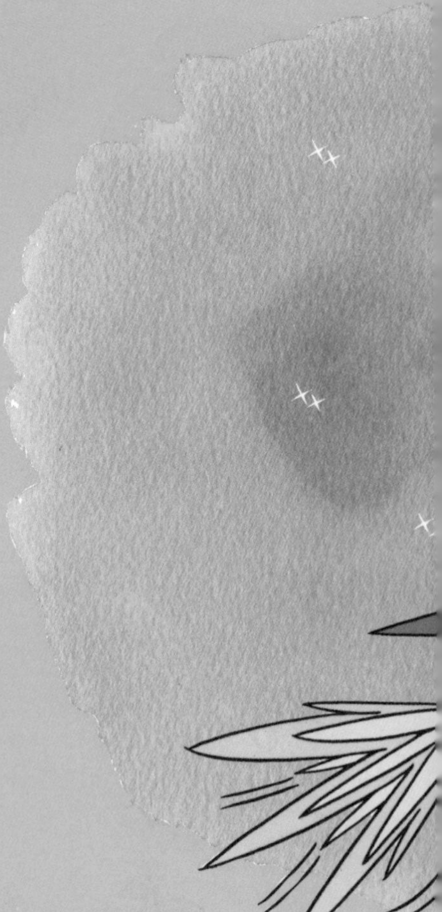

恭喜你！现在你已经能够掌握本书所提到的各种神奇的记忆工具了。同时也能够掌控记忆力与自我意识了。继续与你的记忆力玩耍吧，它会帮助你记住每件你想记住的事情。而且最重要的是，你能记住所有的事情！

你的学习与记忆容量没有上限。这表示你能达到的境界永无止境！

你所使用的思维导图，还有其他记忆工具都具有魔法杖一般神奇的威力。

它们可以成为你一辈子的朋友，帮助你，让你的记忆力更好，让你在学习时更专心。少一点压力，让老师对你刮目相看；成为考试高手，让同学们惊羡不已。你会知道自己可以变得多么优秀。

你正在加入一个在全球拥有上万名会员的俱乐部，这些会员都在使用了思维导图和其他记忆工具之后获得了巨大成功。

这些方法能让你对各类状况都应付自如，发挥出自己的最佳智力、获得高分，表现得出类拔萃——这是你应得的人生！

就在今天，把你的聪明才智发挥到极致吧！